Good Food

Simply Prepared

A Collection of Recipes
from 3 Generations of the Styrna Family

Good Food

Simply Prepared

A Collection of Recipes from 3 Generations of the Styrna Family

By Joan Styrna

Illustrated by Sheila Lemieux

PETER E. RANDALL PUBLISHER LLC
2005

ISBN: 0-9771986-4-2

Library of Congress Control Number: 2005908074

Additional books are available from:

Porusta Publisher
213 North Road
Brentwood NH 03833
(603) 770-4023

Produced by:
Peter E. Randall Publisher LLC
Portsmouth NH 03802
www.perpublisher.com

Book Design: Grace Peirce

To my Mom and Dad

Anne and Stanley Styrna,
Whose love, guidance and wisdom
Allowed me to soar in a multitude of ways.
I love you.

Acknowledgments

My gratitude to Brian Deveney, Matthew Morrison, Jenifer Pellerin, Marilyn and George Prell, Barbara Simon, Maggie Simon, Scott Strainge, and Peg and Marty Stout for tasting and critiquing my recipes.

A special thank you to Sheila Lemieux for your illustrations, which capture perfectly the essence of my recipes.

A very special thank you to my longtime friends and editors, Peg and Marty Stout, for your encouragement, guidance, and professionalism—without you, this book could not have been written.

Thank you to everyone who shared your recipes and stories of your personal heritage.

≋ Contents

✺ Introduction

*A*lthough it takes many different forms, creativity is an essential part of every person's life. For me, it was sparked as a young child by an intense interest in cooking. Early on, I remember watching Julia Child's *Mastering the Art of French Cooking* on television. Although her cookbook was too advanced for me at the time, I was inspired by her passion for cooking. I began collecting editions of Betty Crocker cookbooks, which had recipes that were easy for the amateur cook, as they contained pictures illustrating the procedures and final products. Before the age of ten, my own passion for cooking developed and I started my life's journey, following this creative endeavor to where I am now.

The collection of Betty Crocker cookbooks has now grown to a personal library of more than four hundred cookbooks; my interest in watching cooking shows on television has expanded to giving my own cooking demonstrations; and after starting with baking simple cookies, my repertoire now includes gourmet foods that require the skill and knowledge that come from years of experience.

With a bachelor's degree in home economics and coursework at Madeleine Kamman's Modern Gourmet Boston, the San Francisco Culinary Academy, and New York's Culinary Institute of America, I have pursued careers as a teacher and a chef. After eight years as a sous- and pastry chef, I took my life's experiences and brought them to a high school classroom in southern New Hampshire. For more than fifteen years I have taught students how to prepare good food through the operation of a faculty dining room and district catering service.

The enthusiastic response and participation of the faculty and staff to a gourmet dining room has been overwhelming. Faculty, students, and their parents frequently ask for recipes to dishes being served in addition to recipes for personal use. Over the years, I have been asked countless times when I was going to write a cookbook. Finally I began to consider the idea, and started to collect my favorite recipes, enjoying reminiscing about how I had obtained them.

Once when I asked friends over for dinner, they asked me to

select a menu reflecting my heritage. During that dinner, the conversation centered on the intrigue of the history associated with family recipes and food traditions. The exchange of stories that evening inspired me to write my personal history along with the recipes with the hope that my stories will bring enjoyment to others. In this way, I would create a book that would reflect my life and career, my memoirs.

Good Food Simply Prepared is a different type of cookbook. A collection of recipes from three generations of one family, each chapter has a story depicting the home values and traditions that have influenced the style of food prepared as family members became assimilated into American culture. Many of the recipes have been supplemented with an anecdote or story, and all recipes have been tested for accuracy. Various recipes have been tasted and critiqued by friends who enjoy good food. It is with great pleasure that I share my recipes, my stories, and friends' comments. I hope you enjoy my creative endeavors and find inspiration to spark your own.

CHAPTER ONE

Baba and Grandpa

❄ Baba and Grandpa

*T*he story of my love of *good food, simply prepared* really begins in the 1890s with the birth of my grandparents. It is a story that is connected to the desire for education, a life where there were choices and freedoms, and the preservation of family traditions.

Stanislaw Styrnowski, the eldest of two sons, was born on December 23, 1892, in Belarussia to a blacksmith who made horse-shoes and also farmed, like everyone else in the town. Grandpa learned his father's trade and was proud that he could shoe a horse without getting kicked. In spite of opportunities to follow in his father's footsteps, Grandpa was not happy with the life his country had to offer him. He recognized the importance of education but was frustrated knowing that the rich went to school and the poor did not. At age nineteen, he finally decided that he wanted to go to the United States, where there would be a better life and an opportunity for educating his children. Grandpa's parents recognized their son's dream and worked hard to get together enough money for his trip. The day he left on his journey, Grandpa and his father stood at the railroad station waiting for the train. They hugged each other tight, and when the train started to pull out, Grandpa's father wouldn't let go. Grandpa gently pushed his father away, knowing that he would never see him again. He boarded the moving train, facing a long voyage to America.

Grandpa joined a group of people immigrating to America, many of whom were Jewish. A guide took the group to the country's border and instructed them to stay low as he negotiated with the guards. When he waved, they were to run. The Jewish people, having deep-rooted food traditions, carried on their backs their kitchen utensils, which were dear to them. Grandpa remembered the loud clinking and clanking of these utensils as they ran. The guards obviously heard the noise, but did not fire their guns at them as they crossed the border to the beginning of a new life.

Recently I read the book *Walking on Walnuts*, by Nancy Ring, and enjoyed her description of Jewish ancestors carrying what they could on their backs. As she told the story of the special utensils of

1

her grandmothers and how they were used in the kitchen for holiday celebrations, I wondered if Grandpa realized that his Jewish friends were carrying their heritage with them.

Grandpa's journey took him to Hamburg, to Liverpool, and finally to Ellis Island. When Grandpa arrived in the United States, sometime around 1910, the Industrial Revolution was going strong and needed healthy people to labor in the textile mills. Grandpa settled in Nashua, New Hampshire, and began working at the mills running a napping machine used for woolen blankets. This is where he met his wife.

Elizabeth Juchnevich was born in Grodno, Poland, on April 25, 1895. Her father had a low-paying job for the railroad switching tracks for the trains. While two other children remained in Poland to work the farm, Elizabeth was sent to America because there would be one less mouth for her parents to feed. Arriving at Ellis Island somewhere around 1912, at age sixteen, she made her way to Nashua and found work in the mills. Her job was to replace the spools of thread in the spinning wheels that made blankets.

My grandparents married and had two sons. Their oldest son, Stanley, is my father. Baba (an affectionate name for a grandmother) worked off and on in between children. As the children entered fifth grade, she returned to work full time to save money for her sons' education, and continued until both sons had graduated from college. I acknowledge the hardship my grandparents faced working long, laborious hours to educate their sons and to provide fulfilling lives for their grandchildren, all of whom hold college degrees.

When the economy was slow, work in the mills was sporadic. Feeding a family was a challenge, but Baba was able to make healthy, tasty, and filling meals. There was always soup: cabbage soup, beet soup, potato soup, lentil soup, bean soup, mushroom soup, pea soup, vegetable soup. These were served with a hearty rye bread that was dipped in the soup to fill the stomach cavity.

My interest in good food simply prepared must have been sparked by my dad's stories as well as by remembrances of my grandparents' cooking. As a child, Dad picked mushrooms in the

woods and Baba sautéed them to serve over meats. They picked wild blueberries and canned them for winter use. Dad searched for wild apple trees and brought home fruit for Baba to make various apple dishes. The family picked elderberries and Grandpa made wine in the cellar. They walked along country roads looking for wild grapevines to pick Concord grapes for jelly making and sometimes juice. To this day, Dad and I walk along country roads in Maine picking wild blueberries, raspberries, and blackberries. The family traditions of using as many natural foods from our land as possible continue.

Potatoes, inexpensive and hearty, are always in my memory. Baba and Grandpa bought potatoes by the barrel from a local farmer during the fall harvest and stored them in a cold cellar for the winter. They were fried in bacon fat, made into pancakes, baked as a cake with a crispy crust in a deep spider skillet, baked in the woodstove oven, and mashed by hand with a wooden potato masher. Baba soured her own cream on the kitchen table and served that over boiled potatoes.

In the winter, my grandparents bought a side of pork and cured their own bacon by salting and hanging it in the attic on bamboo poles to dry. Eating meat was a twice-a-week occurrence and consisted of pressed ham, bologna, hamburger, or kielbasa. They ate chicken once a year at Thanksgiving. Baba bought farmer cheese and, as it dried out a bit, fried it in butter and spread it over bread. Grandpa took his sons fishing at nearby ponds for catfish, pickerel, bass, and sunfish and Baba fried them up in cornmeal. Baba had a green fat crock, and all fat drippings went into it for frying foods and making pie dough. Food was never thrown away; any leftovers always showed up in another dish. High-fat foods kept the family warm, fed full, and energized and walking kept the family fit; cars were not affordable in those days.

After retirement, Baba and Grandpa actively maintained a very large garden growing tomatoes and cucumbers, onions and potatoes, winter squash, strawberries and raspberries. They canned and froze and had a cold cellar for winter storage. They made compost

from leaves, kitchen scraps, and old garden plants. This was Grandpa's natural fertilizer and he caught rainwater off the garage roof in a barrel for watering his garden. All his fruits and vegetables tasted the way produce ought to taste, totally natural.

Baba and Grandpa worked hard, saved, and spent wisely. They used, reused, and recycled to attain the goal for which they came to America: to provide a better life for them, their children, and their grandchildren through education. Baba and Grandpa led relatively healthy lives until their deaths at age ninety-nine and eighty-seven, respectively. They have always been an inspiration to me. They have taught me and shared with me the family traditions of which food was such a large part; additionally, the way they lived their lives has given me the opportunity to live my life independently, with freedom to make choices for the happiness of a good life, simply lived.

Food Cooked on the Woodstove

I have a fondness for an old kitchen woodstove my grandparents had in their cellar. It had a large oven, making it a very versatile stove. When we visited on weekends, Grandpa fired up the stove and cooked us dinner.

Thanksgiving dinners are a special remembrance. Grandpa would be up at 3 a.m. to light the fire. The turkey went into the oven an hour later and roasted slowly all morning. Potatoes, squash, turnips, and onions simmered slowly on the stove's surface. The aromas filling the house as the family arrived were heavenly. Food always tasted so good.

When Baba and Grandpa passed on, my parents brought the woodstove and its memories to their cellar for our continued enjoyment. Dad jazzed things up by laying a carpet in front of the stove, positioning three cushioned rocking chairs, and building a dining table made out of two-by-fours. The cellar became the family's retreat.

Learning how to cook on a woodstove was an adventure. New Year's Eve, I made pizza and baked it on the floor of the woodstove oven. Bread dough rose on the back shelf of the woodstove and

later baked in the oven. Baked potatoes came out browned and crispy. When the burners were removed from the stove, a wok sat in place for stir-fries. Soups were simmered slowly on the back of the stove and if we got hungry, the soup was always there waiting for us.

You've never had toast if you haven't made it on top of a wood-stove. Once the stovetop is hot, at least 400°F, place bread slices on top and toast to your desired darkness. I like to see the smoke burning through the toast; it adds such flavor. Toast both sides of the bread and remove with a spatula. Butter the toast and enjoy!

Cook's Tips:

Buy a thermometer that measures the degrees of heat on your woodstove. You can find one at a woodstove dealer. You will be able to control the cooking a little easier if you know the degrees.

Cabbage Soup

My family enjoys the broth in this soup, by soaking it up with a piece of hearty, dark rye bread.

3 pounds beef blade roast
1 large carrot, diced
1 large onion, diced
$1/4$ cup celery, diced
2 bay leaves
1 tablespoon salt
$1^1/_2$ teaspoons pepper
1 head cabbage, chopped
2 cups crushed tomatoes
2 tablespoons apple cider vinegar

Place the beef roast in a soup pot and cover with cold water. Slowly bring to a boil, skimming off the foam as it rises to the top. Add the carrot, onion, celery, bay leaves, salt, and pepper. Simmer, partially covered, for 2 hours. Remove the beef and set aside to cool.

Add the diced cabbage, tomatoes, and vinegar to the soup and simmer another $1^1/_2$ to 2 hours, until the cabbage is thoroughly cooked.

Remove the meat from the bones. Add the meat to the soup and discard the bones. Remove the bay leaves, and adjust the salt, pepper, and vinegar to taste. Serve hot.

Makes 6–8 servings

GOOD FOOD SIMPLY PREPARED

Cook's Tips:

Always use beef with a bone for soups; the bones add a lot of flavor.

Beef shanks are another good cut of meat to use for soups.

When preparing beef and bones for soup, start out with cold water and slowly bring it to a boil. Impurities in the meat will rise to the surface and can be skimmed off. Doing this is not necessary but produces a more refined soup.

Critic's Comments:

This delightfully healthy soup is very mild yet slightly tangy. The acidity of the tomatoes is beautifully offset by the carrots, which add a light sweetness to the broth. The beef is delectably tender and wonderfully complemented by the cabbage. A grand accompaniment to this dish would be fresh sourdough bread with a generous helping of butter.

—Jenifer Pellerin

Hot Beet Soup

Grandpa grew an abundance of beets in his garden and stored them in a cold cellar for use in both hot and cold beet soups.

3 pounds beef stew meat
1 large onion, diced
1 tablespoon salt
1^1/$_2$ teaspoons pepper
4 bay leaves
8 medium-size beets with greens
^{1}/$_4$ cup apple cider vinegar
1 cup sour cream

Place the stew beef in a soup pot and cover with water about 2 inches over the meat. Slowly bring to a boil, skimming the residue off the top.

Add the onion, salt, pepper, and bay leaves. Reduce to a simmer.

Cut the greens from the beets. Wash the leaves and cut into shreds. Peel the beets and cut into julienne. Add the leaves and beet strips to the soup pot. Add the vinegar and simmer, partially covered, for 2 to 3 hours, or until the meat is tender. Remove the bay leaves.

Finish the soup with sour cream and adjust the vinegar, salt, and pepper to taste.

Makes 6–8 servings

Cook's Tips

For greater flavor, use beef with a bone, and remove the bone before serving.

Pork with a bone can be used in place of beef.

Choose beets that are small to medium in size. Large beets can be woody in the center.

The beet greens are nutritious and delicious. Include these in the soup or serve them as a side dish.

Critic's Comments

A constant fan of beets, I can say that I have never been happier than when I sat on a cold winter day with this soup. The mercury hovered around zero as I heated up this warm and deep-colored soup. The beef was tender and marinated with beet juice, and as the aroma filled the kitchen, I was warm and snug with soup I found to be much heartier than expected. I highly recommend this celebration of beets.

—Brian Deveney

Grandpa's Stuffed Cabbage Rolls

Our summer cottage is more than one hundred years old, very crooked, with many cracks and holes for the littlest creature's to crawl through. We were having trouble cooking meat dishes during the daytime because they drew many flies. My mom came up with the idea of cooking at night while the flies were sleeping. We put our cabbage rolls into a 225°F oven just before retiring for the night, and took them out the next morning, about eight hours later. This was our secret technique for great cabbage rolls: long, slow cooking. They were soft as butter. Even without flies, this is how we cook cabbage rolls today.

1^1/$_2$ cups rice	1 tablespoon pepper
1^1/$_2$ cups water	1 tablespoon marjoram
1 teaspoon salt	1 tablespoon oregano
1 extra-large head cabbage	1 tablespoon sage
3 pounds hamburger	1 teaspoon nutmeg
2 pounds ground pork	3 eggs
2 large onions, finely diced	6 slices bacon
2 tablespoons salt	1 can (10^1/$_2$ ounce) tomato soup

Cook the rice in the water and salt until the water is absorbed. Set aside to cool.

Preheat the oven to 300°F.

Bring a large pot of salted water to a boil. Using a long tined fork, stab the core end of the cabbage and lower the leaves into the water. Carefully cut away the leaves, allowing them to parboil a bit until slightly wilted about one minute. Remove and cool.

Finely chop the remainder of the cabbage and place in a large mixing bowl. Add the hamburger, pork, rice, and the onions. Add the salt and pepper and the spices and combine. Incorporate the eggs and mix well.

Lay each cabbage leaf flat. Place a handful of the hamburger mixture at the base of each leaf and fold up, sides in, like a pocket. Arrange half of these cabbage rolls in the bottom of a large roasting pan. Season with salt and pepper, then lay three slices of the bacon on top. Arrange the rest of the cabbage rolls atop the first layer and season with salt and pepper.

Spread the tomato soup evenly over the top and lay the last three slices of bacon on top.

Cover and bake for 5 hours. Remove the cover and cook for another hour to brown.

Makes 20–25 cabbage rolls

Cook's Tips

This is an easy recipe, but time consuming. Congregate the family and make plenty of cabbage rolls for the freezer for those nights you don't have time to cook.

Many recipes for cabbage rolls call for just salt and pepper, but it is the combination of the herbs that makes this recipe special.

Add a small can of cranberry sauce to the tomato soup before spreading on top of the cabbage rolls. Sensational!

Critics' Comments

Cabbage had just the right flavor and body. The meat in the stuffing had just enough moistness to hold together and still not fall apart. The sauce was so tasty that we would love to have even more to add on top. This stuffed cabbage was even beautiful to look at; it could be placed on fine china for a real gourmet presentation!

—George and Marilyn Prell

Kotleti

Kotleti is Russian for hamburger. It bears no resemblance to the American hamburger served medium rare with cheese in a bun.

1^1/$_2$ pounds 85% ground beef
^{1}/$_2$ cup finely diced green peppers
^{1}/$_2$ cup finely diced onion
2 eggs
6 saltines, coarsely crushed
1 teaspoon salt
^{1}/$_2$ teaspoon pepper

Mix all ingredients thoroughly. Shape into 5-ounce patties about 1^1/$_2$ inches thick.

Sauté in a little olive oil over medium low heat, covered, until cooked through, 8 to 10 minutes on each side.

Makes 5 patties

Cook's Tips

85% ground beef produces a moister patty, but you can use 95% ground beef if you want to be more health conscious.

Shape a large meatball and flatten it slightly. Keep the shape of the patties thick.

The patties should feel moist with egg before they are cooked. This creates the right texture.

Serve patties as is or topped with sautéed mushrooms in gravy.

Critic's Comments

Leave the ketchup in the fridge when you dig into this great twist on the traditional hamburger. This burger practically explodes with flavor. My favorite ingredient is the saltines. When I first saw them on the ingredient list I was skeptical, but believe me, they soak up the juices to provide a moist burst of flavor with almost every bite.

—Matt Morrison

Babka

This is a Lithuanian babka—a potato cake—made from grated raw potatoes and onions. Grandpa made this almost every time my sister and I came to visit. He baked it in the woodstove oven, so it came out brown with a thick crust. My mom made a babka on Saturday nights and timed it to come out of the oven when *The Jackie Gleason Show* began. A favorite family pastime was to watch the show and devour the crispy potato cake.

$2/3$ cup bacon drippings, butter, or oil
6 or 7 medium potatoes, about $2^1/_2$ lbs
1 large onion
2 eggs
$1/_4$–$1/_2$ cup flour
1 tablespoon salt
$1^1/_2$ teaspoons pepper
sour cream (optional)

Preheat the oven to 425°F.

Spoon the bacon drippings in a 10-inch heavy skillet and melt over medium heat. Get the skillet quite hot.

Using a food processor with the blade, puree the potatoes and onion. Transfer to a bowl and add the eggs, flour, salt, and pepper.

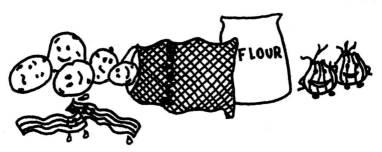

Pour most of the bacon drippings into the potato batter and stir until almost incorporated; leave a little fat on top. Return the skillet to the burner to keep hot.

Pour the potato batter into the hot skillet. Bake for 15 to 20 minutes, then reduce the heat to 400°F and bake for 1 hour, or until the crust is thick, crispy, and brown. Serve plain or with sour cream, if using.

Makes 8 servings as a side dish

Cook's Tips

Bake the babka in a cast-iron skillet. Cast iron retains heat and creates a great crust.

Check the moisture of the potatoes you are using and determine how much flour you'll need. Watery or new potatoes need more flour.

Bacon drippings make the best babka, but you can use half drippings and half butter or half drippings and half oil.

Potatoes cooked with fat should be brown and crispy, so cook at a higher heat.

Purchase smokehouse bacon and use the drippings for cooking and frying. The flavor is superior.

Critics' Comments

A rich-tasting potato dish with varying textures, the babka is a meal in itself or an excellent accompaniment to a meat or chicken dish. It is crispy on the outside and moist and soft on the inside, creating a perfect blend of flavors.

—Peg and Marty Stout

Fried Potatoes

Baba sometimes added sliced kielbasa to the frying potatoes, and served sauerkraut on the side. Potatoes fried in bacon drippings are delicious. Use a medium high-heat to make them crispy.

Bacon drippings
2 pounds potatoes, peeled and thinly sliced
Salt and pepper
1 pound kielbasa, sliced (optional)

Heat a skillet on medium high. Melt enough bacon drippings to cover the bottom of the skillet by $1/4$ inch.

When the drippings are hot, add the potatoes, season with the salt and pepper, cover, and fry about 40 minutes, turning occasionally. Uncover, add the sliced kielbasa, if using, and fry another 20 minutes, or until brown and crispy on both sides, stirring frequently.

Makes 6 servings as a side dish, 4 servings as a main dish

Cook's Tips

Do not cover potatoes while they are browning; they will become soggy.

Add a sliced onion with the kielbasa to the frying potatoes. Just be sure to keep the skillet hot for browning and crisping.

Add more kielbasa for a heartier main dish.

Chłodnik

Baba made this salad often throughout the year, especially during the summer. The dressing is very liquid and this dish could be served as cold soup. A European-style salad, this is one of my favorites!

1 pint sour cream
2 cups whole milk
Salt and pepper
1 head iceberg lettuce
2 cucumbers, peeled, quartered lengthwise, and cut into cubes
1 bunch scallions, diced

Whisk together the sour cream, milk, salt, and pepper to taste.

Tear the lettuce into bite-size pieces. Add the lettuce, cucumber cubes, and scallions to the sour cream mixture. Mix thoroughly.

Let stand for several hours in the refrigerator, stirring frequently. Serve cold.

Makes 6 servings

Cook's Tips

Substituted one small-diced sweet onion for the scallions.

Reduced fat sour cream can be used along with skim milk, but reduce the amount of milk to 1 cup.

The amount of sour cream and milk can be adjusted to your tastes.

Critic's Comments

One thing I can guarantee about this salad is that it is unlike any you've ever tried before. It's actually a lot like soup in consistency and texture. What I like about it is the soggy lettuce and the kick from the scallions. I can't say that it is one of my favorites, but you should definitely give it a try if you're looking to expand your salad repertoire or if you want a truly unique salad experience.

—Matt Morrison

Colored Easter Eggs with Horseradish

The big event on Easter Sunday is an egg fight, using specially colored eggs. Someone holds his egg with the pointed end up while someone else taps it with the pointed end of her egg. The winner must break both pointed ends of the egg. Now the next person battles the winner. Eventually, everyone is eliminated except for the champion. Sometimes we use our winning egg until it is broken.

One year Grandpa kept winning all the fights. The family was baffled. Our frustrations were building and we were determined to beat him. After a day of losing egg fight after egg fight, Mom found Grandpa's egg; it was made of glass!

After all the fights and broken eggshells, the eggs are peeled and eaten with a mound of horseradish. Here's how to color your eggs.

On Ash Wednesday we start saving onionskins, the papery outsides of the onion. Save enough skins to fill one vegetable bin in the refrigerator. To make the dye, a few days before Easter, put the skins in a 4-quart pot, cover with water, and boil for 10 minutes. This process extracts the color from the skins and turns the water a deep-orange brown. Let this colored water sit at room temperature overnight and do not drain.

Eggshells are porous; your Easter eggs will pick up a slight onion flavor and the shells will turn various shades of red-orange-brown.

Place twelve eggs at a time in the colored water, nestled within the onionskins. Bring the water to a boil, then simmer for 5 minutes. Remove the eggs and run under cold water. We color four-dozen eggs: one dozen for ourselves, the rest for family and friends.

Horseradish is an important staple made from the ground roots. These roots are so hot that peeling and grating are done outdoors or in the garage with the door open. Even then, the tears can become unbearable and the family must take turns grating the root. Add a little distilled white vinegar to prevent the roots from discoloring. Pack the horseradish into small jars; save some for Easter, and freeze the rest to serve with meats later on.

Farmer cheese is fashionable around Easter. Baba bought farmer cheese by the 3-pound block. The cheese was left unwrapped in the refrigerator for several days to dry out. It was then sliced into $1/2$-inch pieces and fried in butter. The cheese melts and becomes gooey and stringy. The family ate it as is or spread it on rye bread. Farmer cheese cooked this way is absolutely delicious!

Cook's Tips

Depending on how many onions you use in cooking, start saving onionskins when you think appropriate.

Always simmer eggs—boiling will make them tough and rubbery.

Running hard cooked-eggs under cold water produces a layer of steam between the egg and shell, making it easier to peel.

Use eggs that are close to two weeks old; really fresh eggs don't peel easily.

Farmer cheese is a low-fat, healthy cheese and I substitute it for cottage and ricotta cheeses in many recipes.

You can fry farmer cheese in olive oil, but butter has a nicer flavor.

Lithuanian Pierogi

Grandpa made Lithuanian pierogi every Easter and occasionally throughout the year. Easter breakfast is a piece of pierogi slathered in butter and eaten with boiled eggs and horseradish. This bread is definitely a family favorite and one I want to enjoy always. Grandpa gave me three versions of his recipe to interpret and this one is the best. On the following pages are my grandpa's original recipes. I truly cherish them, as they are in his own handwriting and language.

    2 tablespoons dry yeast
    2 cups warm whole milk
    3 cups bread flour
    2 teaspoons salt

Dissolve the yeast in the warm milk. Beat in the flour and salt and let rest for 5 hours in a warm place. You are making what is called a sponge.

    1 cup sugar
    1 stick salted butter, softened
    3 eggs
    2 pounds golden raisins
    3 to 4 cups flour

Add the sugar, butter, eggs, raisins, and 3 cups of the flour to the sponge.

Knead the dough for 10 minutes, gradually working in the last cup of flour. The dough should be sticky without sticking to your hands.

Butter two soufflé dishes. Divide the dough in half and shape

loaves into rounds. Place into the soufflé dishes and cover with a towel. Let the bread rise until double in bulk, about two hours.

Bake in a 300°F oven for 90 minutes. Remove to a wire rack and rub the crusts with butter and allow to cool.

Makes 2 round loaves

Cook's Tips

Use bread flour for better texture.

Use a mixer with a dough hook for easier kneading.

Critic's Comments

The semi-firm texture softly dissolves when eaten. It has just the right blend of spices and number of raisins. There's no need for butter!

—Marilyn Prell

how to made Lithuanian piragas
or cake

made half quart warm milk
one yeast cake melt in the milk
put one pound flour
tea spoon salt
half cup Sugar
2 eggs
quarter pound magarine and mix
All to getter then keep in warm place
5 or 6 hours

then put one package Raisins and add
more flour and knead to getter if
paste stick to the hand put little
more flour not to much make paste
soft and smooth

then put little magarine in the Dish
And smear or rub with magarine Dish
And put paste in the Dish and keep in
warm place when paste get up
Became ful Dish then put in the
oven 300 Degree one hour
And be Ready

to be one Big cake could divide make 2

this is second prescription how to made
Lithuanian piragas or cake

put half quart warm milk 2 C.
a yeast cake melt in the milk
put one and half pound flour 3 cups
a tea spoon salt
And mix all to getter then keep in warm
place 5 hours after

then put cup sugar
quarter pound of magarine or more
3 Eggs Beaden
one and half package Raisins and
Add more flours then Knead to getter 3-4 c.
if paste stick to the hand put more
flour not to much make paste
saft and smooth

then put little magarine in the Dish and
Rub with magarine Dishes then put paste
in the Dishes and keep in the warm place
when paste get up Become ful Dishes
then put in the oven 300. Degree
one hour and be Ready

Divide

Apple Blini

Blini is the Polish term for pancake. Baba made these thin apple pancakes for dinner often during the Depression. This is a simple crêpe batter to which thinly sliced apples have been added, then the pancake is fried in butter. Back in those days, butter was readily available and relatively inexpensive. These blinis are served simply as is.

I often think of one particular cold snowy night. Dad fired up the woodstove in the cellar. We sensed that the next day would be a non-work day and we braced for the inconvenience of a nor'easter. We checked our flashlights, filled water jugs, and prepared for a power outage. We settled in our rockers, popping our feet into the woodstove oven. Dad opened a bottle of "cold duck" sparkling wine. We sipped, we talked, and we laughed! Mom made apple blinis on the woodstove; we ate off our laps and washed them down with a little more "cold duck." We floated off to a serene night's sleep. We often reminisce about that night and the simple joy it brought us.

2 cups flour
2 cups whole milk
2 eggs
$1/4$ teaspoon salt
4 Cortland apples, peeled, cored, and thinly sliced
Butter

Beat together the flour, milk, eggs, and salt and let stand for 15 minutes. Stir the apples into the batter.

Set a sauté pan on medium heat and melt butter to coat. Spoon two tablespoons of the mixture with apples into the pan and fry the pancakes until golden brown, about 3 minutes on each side.

These blinis can be eaten with maple syrup and served for brunch or lunch.

Makes 25 pancakes 3 inches in diameter

Cook's Tips

It is best to use butter in this recipe; that's where the flavor is.

Fry in half butter and half oil to reduce the saturated fat.

Use a hand-crank apple peeler to peel, core, and slice the apples. It works well, and is easy and relatively inexpensive.

This is a great meal for children.

Baba's Sweet Applesauce Pudding

3 cups cooked rice
3 eggs
1^1/$_2$ cups whole milk
^{1}/$_2$ cup sugar
1^1/$_2$ teaspoons cinnamon
^{1}/$_4$ teaspoon nutmeg
^{1}/$_2$ teaspoon vanilla
5 cups Homemade Applesauce (see page 30)

Preheat the oven to 400°F.

Butter a 3-quart casserole. Spread the cooked rice over the bottom of the casserole.

Beat together the eggs, milk, sugar, cinnamon, nutmeg, and vanilla. Stir this mixture evenly into the rice.

Cover the top with an inch or so of applesauce, then bake for 30 minutes, or until a paring knife inserted in the middle comes out clean. Serve plain or with whipped cream.

Makes 12 one cup servings

Cook's Tips

Before cooking the rice, rinse it in a strainer under cold running water until the water runs clear. This process removes excess starch.

Cook 1 cup of rice in 2 cups of water with a dash of salt until the water is absorbed, about 20 minutes. This will yield 3 cups of cooked rice.

Critic's Comments

The pudding was good, even better when warmed slightly. My husband, George, added whipped cream on his *second* helping. I sprinkled some cinnamon on mine. It reminded me of a true old-fashioned pudding—not a jello packaged one!

—Marilyn Prell

Homemade Applesauce

Making your own applesauce is so easy and has a wonderful taste. This recipe makes enough applesauce for Baba's Applesauce Pudding.

10 Cortland apples
1 cup water
3/4 cup brown sugar
2 teaspoons cinnamon
1 1/2 teaspoons vanilla
Juice of half a lemon

Peel, core, and dice the apples. Place the apples in a deep pot and cover with the water; cook over medium heat until the apples are soft and falling apart, about 1 hour. Remove from heat.

Add the cinnamon, vanilla and lemon juice and stir to combine. Serve warm or cold or make Baba's Applesauce Pudding.

Makes 5 one cup servings

Cook's Tips

Use a hand-crank apple peeler to peel, core, and slice the apples. It works well, and is easy and relatively inexpensive.

I like the flavor intensity of brown sugar, but white sugar is fine, too.

Always use real vanilla. Add it after the applesauce has been removed from the heat; it scorches easily, and gives a burnt taste.

Lemon juice brings out the natural flavor of the apples. Always use fresh lemons.

For a smooth applesauce, add the sugar at the end of cooking. For a chunky applesauce, add the sugar at the beginning of cooking.

how to made a raisins bread.
1 quart hot milk
2 pound flaur
2 teas spoon salt
and now mix all together
add dissolvet a 2 yesat cake in little
warm milk and add to the mix ture.
now put mixture in warm place
for 5 hours. after that
   add 1 cup sugar.
and   dissolve 1 stick margarine
and 2 eggs beaten and 1 packag raisins
and 1 pound flaur.
and mix all ingredints to gether.
after that knead good all ingredints
if paste stick to the hand put
more flaur but not to much make
paste soft and smooth.
devide in two and then greass two
pans and brush tops with beaten
egg and place in a warm oven ur
it raises to the top of pan. bake in moder
oven (300°) for 1 hour

CHAPTER TWO

Mom and Dad

☀ Mom and Dad

Although I never knew my maternal grandparents—they passed away before I was born—they, too, were instrumental in shaping my passion for cooking. Like my dad's parents, George Porusta and Mary Smarega left Poland and came to America in search of opportunities to make a better living. They both found employment in the mills of Nashua, New Hampshire, and met soon after.

George and Mary's wedding reception was held at a friend's boarding house. At the time, Grandpa Styrna was a boarder living upstairs, listening to the roaring celebration; the next day he inquired about the newlyweds. Little did Grandpa Styrna know that his son Stanley would someday marry George and Mary's youngest daughter, Anne. Stanley and Anne are my parents.

After years of raising their families and living across town from each other, the Styrnas and Porustas moved into the same neighborhood on Perry Avenue in Nashua. Sharing a similar heritage, they soon became very good friends.

Anne Porusta, my mother, was studying hairdressing in Boston and practiced on Baba's hair. One evening Anne was doing Baba's hair and Stanley, my dad, was home on furlow from the U.S. Army; he offered to walk Mom home and invited her to the movies that Sunday. The next time they saw each other was on the train to Boston; Mom was going to school and Dad was returning to the military.

A year later, Mom received a Christmas card from overseas. Excited that it was from her boyfriend, Jerry, she opened the card and to her disappointment it was signed *Stanley*.

Dad was discharged from the service in February 1946 and began spending time at the Porusta household. For a while it was not clear whether Dad was courting Mom or her older sister, Agnes. Then Dad began taking Mom out to the movies and on walks around Silver Lake on Sundays. Their courtship was growing.

In May 1946, Dad went to Delaware to begin work in engineering. A railroad strike was in progress and Dad could not get back to Nashua to propose marriage to Mom, so he proposed in writing.

Mom wrote back, "We will discuss it when you get home." Two weeks later, in June, Dad got home and immediately spoke of marriage. Mom instantly replied, "I will, I will, I will"—end of discussion!

That July, while visiting Mom's sister, Francis, in Fitchburg, Massachusetts, they found an ad in the local newspaper for engineers at the General Electric Company. Dad went to the plant, applied, and was hired the same day. With the help of my aunt Francis, Mom and Dad rented an apartment together in West Fitchburg and Dad began working for General Electric in mid-August. On September 14, 1946, Mom and Dad were married. They took a weekend honeymoon in Boston and began their life together.

Newly married, Mom started cooking on a small two-burner gas tabletop. Mom and Dad were both working and often met at a local restaurant for a large meal at noon, keeping suppers light. Suppers were simple: chipped beef on rice, fried pressed ham, fried steak with onions, beans and hotdogs. So soon after the war, new stoves with ovens were still unavailable. Once a week Mom's landlord would fire up his oil-burning oven and offer it to her for baking breads or preparing a roast. My parents looked forward each week to their "baking day."

On their first anniversary, Dad gave Mom the Fanny Farmer Cookbook. Inscribed on the inside is "To my lovely wife on our first wedding anniversary." Mom still cherishes this book.

After a year and a half of marriage, my sister, Christine, was born and my parents bought their first home, on White Street in Lunenburg, Massachusetts. I was born four years later. Mom's focus was on her family and new home. My parents remodeled the kitchen and bought their first electric stove. Mom loved to cook and our next-door neighbor, Bertha Sector, enhanced her cooking talents.

Mom met "Mama" Sector when she and Dad moved to White Street. Mama was French and German and had learned to cook from her mother and grandmother. Mom frequently had morning coffee with Mama and then sat at the kitchen table watching Mama cook. Mama was a great baker and always offered her pastries with coffee

to anyone stopping by to visit. Mom's interest in cooking intensified as she copied down recipe after recipe while Mama cooked. There was a twenty-five-year age difference between Mom and Mama, yet they built a strong friendship, one that lasted nearly forty years, ending only when Mama Sector passed away, at age eighty-nine.

Mama Sector's French and German background as well as her ease in baking had a great influence on my mom's knowledge and style of cooking. To this day, Mom is an incredibly creative cook; she can take what is available in her kitchen and prepare wonderful-tasting meals that are simple and inexpensive. The following selections are some of Mom's favorite recipes, with a few of Mama Sector's, also.

Mama Sector Eggs

Mama made this egg dish for her lunch every day for as long as I knew her. She would roll it up and eat it like a sandwich.

1 teaspoon butter
2 eggs
1 slice bread, buttered on one side

Heat a 6-inch nonstick sauté pan over medium-low heat. Add a teaspoon of butter and melt. Crack the eggs into the pan and immediately place the bread, buttered-side up, on top of the eggs. When the eggs are almost set, gently flip them over and turn the heat up to high. Toast the bread to your desired doneness, then slide it, eggs and all, onto a plate.

Makes 1 serving

Cook's Tips

Place the bread onto raw eggs so it will adhere to the egg whites.

Be careful when flipping the eggs so you don't break the yolks, unless you like your eggs that way. Slide a wide spatula under the eggs for easier flipping.

Place four to six slices of pepperoni on top of the eggs before the bread and flip when the eggs are set.

Place a piece of prosciutto and a slice of cheese on top of the eggs before the bread and flip when the eggs are set.

Dad's Famous Scrambled Eggs

Dad never cooked, but he has always helped in preparation of the family meals. He will peel potatoes, carrots, and onions; shuck clams for chowder; roll stuffed cabbage leaves; and knead bread dough. Once when Mom was sick, Dad made scrambled eggs. They were soft and creamy, absolutely delicious! I look forward to Thursdays, when Dad makes his Famous Scrabbled Eggs for breakfast.

1 tablespoon butter
4 eggs

Using an 8-inch nonstick skillet, melt the butter over medium heat. Crack the eggs and drop into the pan. Using a regular teaspoon, scramble the eggs until soft and creamy.

Makes 2 servings

Dad's Tips

Splurge and use real butter.

Be patient and cook eggs over medium heat; high heat makes the eggs dry and rubbery.

Use a regular teaspoon to scramble the eggs; the small spoon keeps the egg curds small.

Sauerkraut and Pork

Mama Sector taught my mom how to make this German version of sauerkraut and pork. This is a family favorite served simply with boiled potatoes.

I was raised on sauerkraut; it's comfort food for me. Columbus Day weekend is the end of our summer season in Maine and one of our last trips is to Morse's Sauerkraut House in Union. The kraut house is open only for a short time in the fall when the cabbages are maturing and ready for processing into sauerkraut. There are acres upon acres of cabbages surrounding the kraut house, a quaint old brick building suitable for fermentation, and you can experience the smell of sauerkraut in the air.

A deli offers a variety of wursts, breads, cheeses, and other German specialties. The kraut house takes Vermont's Cabot Cheddar and ages it for another two years, which produces a magnificently flavored and crystallized cheese. This cheese can easily be served on its own or with crackers; it also makes an outstanding macaroni and cheese.

We never leave the kraut house without a large crusty roll stuffed with a bratwurst, seasoned with spicy mustard and garnished with lots of steaming sauerkraut. We head down to a nearby lake to enjoy our lunch along with the brightly colored foliage. It is always a day to remember.

5 pounds pork roast with bone
1 large onion, diced
2 tablespoons chopped dill
1 tablespoon salt
$1/2$ teaspoon pepper
2 quarts sauerkraut
2 tablespoons caraway seeds
1 large raw potato, grated

Place the pork roast in a deep

stockpot. Cover the meat with cold water. Slowly bring the water to a boil, skimming off the foam as it rises to the surface. When the foam subsides, add the onion, dill, salt, and pepper. Cover the stockpot and simmer for 3 hours.

Remove the pork, cool and debone. Reserve the cooking liquid. To the cooking liquid, add the sauerkraut and caraway seeds; simmer for 30 minutes. Return the boned pork to the sauerkraut and simmer an additional 30 minutes. Add the grated potato, stirring into the sauerkraut until it thickens, about five minutes. Adjust the seasonings.

Serve with potatoes boiled in salted water.

Makes 10–12 servings

Cook's Tips

I use a pork shoulder for the flavor that comes from the bone.

I grow dill during the summer, uproot it, and hang it upside down to dry. I place an entire dill stalk or two in the boiling water and remove it before serving. The flavor is intensive and natural.

I measure heaping tablespoons of caraway seed and sometimes add dill seed. Adjust seasonings according to your taste.

Fresh sauerkraut is best. Canned kraut can be quite acidic, so rinse before using.

The grated potato thickens the cooking liquid, and mellows out the acidity of the sauerkraut; please don't omit this step.

Puree the raw potato using the blade in a food processor.

Critic's Comments

Are you sure this is sauerkraut? It's the best-tasting kraut we've ever had—almost sweet! The caraway seeds added a unique and distinctive flavor. Delicious!

—Marilyn Prell

Making Fresh Sauerkraut

My grandpa made sauerkraut in the cool basement of his house. He would shred cabbage using a handmade cabbage shredder and place it in a barrel with layers of salt. He pounded the cabbage using his handmade wooden temper to extract the water, which would help it to ferment into sauerkraut. A sliced apple would be strewn across the cabbage and covered with a plate and a weight.

After a couple of weeks, the kraut was ready. Dad remembers sneaking down cellar and snacking on the sauerkraut as it was fermenting, something I did years later. Baba would simply heat the sauerkraut and serve it with boiled meats or kielbasa fried with potatoes, a dish we frequently serve today.

Through trial and error, I eventually learned how to make sauerkraut, and will make it 25 pounds at a time. I love the aroma in the cellar while it is fermenting.

5 pounds cabbage, shredded
3 tablespoons salt

Place 1$^1/_2$ pounds of the shredded cabbage in a clean plastic bucket and sprinkle with 1 tablespoon of the salt. Using a wooden mallet, pound the cabbage several times; this is called tempering. It breaks down the cell structure of the cabbage, thereby releasing the cabbage juices.

Repeat this process twice.

Place a clean plate on top of the cabbage and weight it down (I use a clean gallon milk container filled with water). Allow the cabbage to ferment for 2 to 3 weeks at 65—70°F. Periodically taste the sauerkraut. When it is to your liking, pack in clean plastic containers and refrigerate until ready to use.

Makes 5 pounds

Cook's Tips

Before weighting down the cabbage for fermentation, add a peeled, cored, and sliced apple. This adds a touch of sweetness and helps the fermentation. The apple will dissolve into the sauerkraut.

Sauerkraut will store in the refrigerator for about 9 months without spoilage.

Fresh sauerkraut does not have to be rinsed before cooking. Rinsing removes some of the acidity and flavor.

Pork Pâté

3 pounds ground pork
1 large onion, finely diced
1 tablespoon cinnamon
2 teaspoons allspice
1 teaspoon nutmeg
2 bay leaves
2 teaspoons salt
$1^1/_2$ teaspoons pepper
$1^1/_2$ cups cold water

Place the pork and onion in a pot, then add the spices and the salt and pepper. Pour in the water and simmer, partially covered, about $1^1/_2$ hours.

Using a potato masher, frequently mash the meat at the beginning of cooking to break apart any lumps of pork. Leave some liquid at the bottom of the pot. This liquid will gel and hold the pâté together.

Remove the bay leaves and pour the pâté into a terrine mold or standard-size loaf pan and refrigerate until cold.

Makes a 3 pound loaf or 8–9 sandwiches

Cook's Tip

Serve on crackers or bread rounds or in a sandwich using good-quality mustard.

Critic's Comments

The aroma alone made my mouth water! The subtle hint of nutmeg made this reminiscent of Swedish meatballs. One of the best pâtés I've had! I served it on Ritz crackers.

—Marilyn Prell

Stuffed Pepper Steaks

1 green pepper, sliced
1 sweet onion, sliced
4 ounces fresh mushrooms, sliced
4 sticks Velveeta cheese, cut the size of large French fries
4 cube steaks, about 2 pounds
1 can (10.5 ounces) cream of mushroom soup
$1^1/_4$ cups sour cream

Preheat the oven to 350°F.

Sauté the pepper, onion, and mushrooms until soft and golden. Cool.

Place a stick of Velveeta down the center of each cube steak. Top off with a spoonful of the pepper mixture. Roll the steak around the filling and place seam-side down in a casserole.

Mix the cream of mushroom soup with the sour cream and pour over the steaks. Cover with aluminum foil and bake for $1^1/_2$ to 2 hours, or until the meat is tender.

Makes 4 servings

Cook's Tip

Any thin cut of steak can be used in this recipe. Thicker steaks can be pounded thinner.

Critic's Comments

If you're in the mood for something new, and like steak and cheese, definitely give this recipe a try. My wife and I loved the combination of the creamy cheese-and-mushroom filling and the hearty yet tender steak.

—Matt Morrison

Mom's Meat Loaf

1¹/₂ pounds ground beef
1 pound ground pork
2 medium onions, diced
1 small can (7 ounces) mushrooms, sliced and drained
1 can (10.5 ounces) cream of mushroom soup
2 eggs
8 saltines, crushed
1 tablespoon salt
1 teaspoon pepper
2 tablespoons Bell's poultry seasoning
1 quart tomatoes, drained
Oregano, for sprinkling

Preheat the oven to 350°F.

Mix thoroughly the ground meats, onions, mushrooms, soup, eggs, saltines, salt, pepper, and poultry seasoning. Press the mixture into a meat loaf pan.

With your hands, crush the tomatoes over the meat loaf. Sprinkle on the oregano. Bake for about 1¹/₂ hours, or until the meat juices run clear.

Makes 6–8 servings

Cook's Tips

All beef or a mixture of ground meats can be substituted.

The mushrooms are optional, but they add nice flavor.

Saltines are best, but bread crumbs work well.

Critic's Comments

I have a special place in my heart for meat loaf. I find myself taste-testing the meat loaf wherever I go. In fact, I am so enamored of the wonderful dish that I ordered it the night I proposed to my girlfriend. It can also be safely said that I am obsessed with any spice I can use to enhance an otherwise dull meal.

When I sat down to eat this meat loaf, I was armed with a potent hot sauce and spice arsenal. I was pleasantly surprised to find that I would eat my entire meal without ever reaching for even the pepper. This meat loaf is a perfect blend of texture and spice. I can only hope that all my friends find this recipe and begin to cook it for me every time I come over for dinner.

—Brian Deveney

Swiss Steak

My mom always bought quality meats from a butcher shop. Every Sunday, Mom made a roast for dinner: roast beef, pot roast, roast pork loin, roast leg of lamb, or roast chicken. Roasts are simple and good and provide leftovers. Occasionally, Mom made Swiss steak with lots of gravy over mashed potatoes.

2 pounds top round steak
2 pounds carrots, cut into chunks
2 large onions, sliced
Salt and pepper
$1/3$ cup flour
$1/3$ cup water

Cut steak into serving size pieces. Place in a deep pot along with the carrots and onions. Sprinkle with salt and pepper and just cover with cold water. Simmer this mixture for $2^{1}/_{2}$ to 3 hours, or until the steak is tender.

Combine the flour and the water. Stir it into the pot and simmer another 15 to 20 minutes, or until the broth has thickened. Adjust the salt and pepper.

Serve over mashed potatoes.

Makes 4–6 servings

Cook's Tip

Use any cut of steak from the round or chuck; these cuts of meat are very flavorful and will become tender due to the long, slow cooking.

Critic's Comments

This recipe revives memories of childhood suppers. It's special enough for Sunday dinner, too!

—Marilyn Prell

Oven-Fried Chicken

My mom's version of fried chicken is to bake it in the oven, which is healthier with less fat.

1 whole chicken cut into parts
Flour
Seasoned salt
Butter
1 cup water

Preheat the oven to 375°F.

Generously butter a baking dish large enough to hold the chicken pieces in one layer. Using a sieve or a strainer, lightly dust the chicken with flour.

Sprinkle the chicken pieces with the seasoned salt and dot the tops with butter. Pour the water down the sides of the pan, being careful not to wash the flour off the chicken.

Basting every 15 minutes, bake for 1 hour, or until the chicken is brown and crispy.

Makes 4 servings

Cook's Tips

Increase the temperature to 400°F for the last 15 minutes to brown the chicken even more.

Dusting the chicken with flour gives the skin a crispy texture while the meat remains moist.

Use any combination of chicken: legs, breasts, thighs, drumsticks, and wings. You can purchase chicken already cut up.

Use any seasoning mix; garlic and herb seasoning is very good.

Substitute olive oil for the butter for a healthier fat.

Baked Stuffed Haddock

Every Friday night Mom cooked fish, usually haddock, scrod or sole. She dusted the fish with flour, Bisquick, or cornmeal, and then fried it in butter. On occasion, Mom made Baked Stuffed Haddock, a recipe she got from a fisherman's wife in Marblehead, Massachusetts. I remember being served this dish at the fisherman's home near the ocean and loving it.

    2 pounds haddock fillets
    3 cups Pepperidge Farm stuffing mix
    2 cans (10.5 ounces) cream of mushroom soup
    2 1/4 cups whole milk
    2 tablespoons butter

Preheat the oven to 375°F.

Butter a 3-quart square casserole dish. Cut each fish fillet into four pieces and place half in the bottom of the casserole. Spoon half the stuffing mix on top of the fish fillets.

Whisk together the mushroom soup and the milk. Pour half this mixture over the stuffing mix. Add another layer of fish, stuffing mix, and mushroom soup; dot with pieces of butter.

Bake for 45 minutes, or until the top is brown and the juices are bubbling.

Makes 6–8 servings

Cook's Tips

Add a small can of mushrooms to the soup mix.

Sole and cod can be used in place of haddock.

Substitute cheddar cheese soup for the mushroom soup.

Use cream in place of milk for a richer texture.

Critic's Comments

I've experienced very few stuffed fish dishes, but this one certainly ranks among the best. I'm not sure how Joan does it, but the haddock and stuffing seem to combine to create not two distinct textures and flavors, but one texture and one flavor that is a pleasant blend of the two. And because the fish is not overpowering, this is a great dish for reluctant fish eaters.

—Matt Morrison

Lobster Newburg

My mom's sister, Vicky, passed this recipe onto my mom, who has made it every year on my birthday since childhood. Mama and Papa Sector customarily joined us for this celebration.

1 quart whole milk
1 cup coffee cream
3 heaping tablespoons flour
1 1/2 sticks salted butter
Salt and pepper
2 pounds lobster meat, cut into medium-size pieces
1 teaspoon paprika
1 cup sherry

Whisk together the milk, coffee cream, and flour. Cook in a double boiler on medium heat, stirring constantly. Add half the butter and season with salt and pepper.

Melt the remaining butter in a sauté pan, and then add the lobster. Add the paprika and stir. Deglaze the pan with the sherry.

Combine the lobster with the cream sauce, mixing well. Adjust the seasoning.

Serve the lobster Newburg over individual patty shells.

Makes 4–6 servings

Baked Mashed Potatoes

My mom freezes leftover mashed potatoes in quart-size bags for a variety of side dishes. To make Baked Mashed Potatoes, defrost enough, then put them in a buttered casserole and dust the top with Parmesan cheese and paprika. Baked at 400°F for 1 hour, or until you have a golden crust.

Mashed Potato Patties

2 cups cold leftover mashed potatoes
2 tablespoons dried onion flakes
1 egg
$1/2$ teaspoon salt
$1/4$ teaspoon pepper
Flour, for dredging

Thoroughly mix together the mashed potatoes, onion flakes, egg, salt, and pepper. Shape into four patties. Carefully dredge the patties in flour. Sauté patties in butter on medium heat until deep golden brown and a crust has formed, about 10 minutes on each side.

Makes 4 servings

Tuna-Noodle Casserole

Tuna-Noodle Casserole sustained me as a child and my mom makes a great casserole. The cheese is her secret ingredient.

1 package (12 ounces) egg noodles
2 cans (6 ounces) albacore tuna
2 cans (10.5 ounces) cream of mushroom soup
1¼ cups milk
2 small cans (7 ounces) sliced mushrooms, optional
1½ pounds Velveeta cheese
Salt and pepper
Seasoned bread crumbs

Preheat the oven to 375°F.

Cook the noodles according to the directions on the package.

Meanwhile, butter a 4-quart square casserole. Drain the tuna and break it up into the bottom of the casserole.

In a saucepan, heat the soup, milk, mushrooms, and cheese. Stir until the cheese melts; season with the salt and pepper.

Drain the noodles and pour them on top of the tuna in the casserole.

Pour the soup mixture over the noodles and combine thoroughly. Sprinkle the bread crumbs over all.

Bake about 30 minutes, or until the cheese is bubbly and the crumbs brown. Note: You can prepare the casserole and refrigerate before baking. To cook, bake for 1 hour at 375°F.

Makes 4–6 servings

Cook's Tips

I like the wide egg noodles, but you can use your favorites.

Use a good-quality white albacore tuna in water.

Critic's Comments

I grew up eating and enjoying this classic dish as prepared by my mother, so if Joan's was going to impress me, it would need to be pretty special. Not surprisingly, it was. Each ingredient complements the others so well that you want to eat the entire casserole. The moist noodles balance the bread crumbs, while the mild mushroom flavors balance the tuna. I enjoyed it with fresh tomato slices on the side. If you make it, you'll wish you made two, and if you make two, you'll wish there was no one else to share it with.

—Matt Morrison

Mom's Maple Baked Beans

2 pounds navy pea beans
1 teaspoon baking soda
3 small ham hocks
1 large onion, diced
$1/2$ cup maple syrup
2–4 tablespoons ketchup
2 teaspoons dry mustard
1 tablespoon salt
1 teaspoon black pepper
2–8 tablespoons brown sugar
$2/3$ cup molasses

Cover the beans with cold water and soak overnight. Drain and discard the water. Cover the beans with fresh cold water. Add the baking soda to the water and parboil the beans for 15 minutes. Drain and discard the water.

Transfer the beans to a Crock-pot®. Add the ham hocks, onion, maple syrup, ketchup, mustard, salt, and pepper.

Dissolve the brown sugar, to taste, in the molasses and add to the beans. Add boiling water enough to cover the beans.

Cook on high for 5 to 6 hours, or until the beans are tender. Add more water to the beans if they become dry.

Makes 8–10 servings

Cook's Tips

Soaking beans overnight and discarding the water removes the chemical substance that promotes intestinal gas.

If you prefer sweeter beans, add up to 8 tablespoons of brown sugar.

Barbecue sauce can be used in place of ketchup. Add up to $1/4$ cup.

Critic's Comments

The maple beans were enough to satisfy even my large dinner appetite. The smoky maple flavor complemented by a hint of meat made my mouth water even as I began to heat up these great beans. I also found them to be a wonderful cold dish when I placed them beside my Saturday-morning eggs.

—Brian Deveney

Thanksgiving Sage Bread Stuffing

My mother's bread stuffing is the best! It is moist and redolent of sage.

1 cup celery, finely diced
1 large onion, finely diced
4 tablespoons butter
4 cups homemade chicken stock
6 slices whole wheat bread
1 package (16 ounces) seasoned stuffing mix
2 tablespoons sage
1 tablespoon Bell's poultry seasoning
1 1/2 teaspoons salt
1 1/2 teaspoons pepper
4 eggs

In a large saucepan, sauté the celery and onion in the butter until soft. Pour in the chicken stock and heat until just warm.

In a large mixing bowl, tear the whole wheat bread into little pieces. Add the stuffing mix and mix well to combine. Pour the chicken stock over the bread and let it stand at room temperature until the bread absorbs the stock, about 5 minutes. Using your fingertips, mush up the bread.

Add the sage, Bell's seasoning, salt, and pepper; taste and adjust. Blend in the eggs, then stuff the bird.

Makes enough to fill an 18-pound turkey

Cook's Tips

You can use any mixture of bread crumbs, white bread, corn bread, and even rye.

Canned chicken stock or bouillon cubes will work, but reduce the salt by half.

Taste the stuffing for seasoning and adjust before you blend in the eggs to avoid salmonella.

Grow sage in the summer garden. Pick the leaves and let them dry. Finely chop in the food processor and bag for winter use.

Use this stuffing for pork chops and fish, such as fillet of sole and haddock.

Baked Onions

Baked Onions are a great side dish and Mom serves them every Thanksgiving.

3 large Spanish onions
Butter
3 slices bread
Garlic powder
1 cup heavy cream

Peel the onions, but do not cut the ends off. Boil the onions 20 to 30 minutes. Test them with a knife; they should be tender. Drain the onions and cool slightly. Gently cut off the ends and cut the onions in half, crosswise. Place cut-side up in a baking dish large enough to hold all the onions snugly in one layer.

Preheat the oven to 350ºF.

Butter one side of each slice of bread and sprinkle garlic powder to your liking. Cut bread into cubes and place on top of the onions.

Pour the heavy cream around the onions and bake for 45 to 50 minutes, or until the bread cubes are browned and the cream is bubbling. Serve with a bit of the cream on top.

Makes 6 servings

Cook's Tips

Make this dish using whole wheat bread, Smart Balance instead of butter, and fat-free half-and-half. It won't be as rich tasting, but it will be healthier for you.

In addition to garlic powder, sprinkle on oregano, basil, thyme, or other herbs to add flavor.

Onions have a high natural sugar content and become sweet when they are cooked.

Critic's Comments

What a surprise these were. I was a little skeptical at first—and really never thought onions could taste this good—but even my wife, who hates onions, loved this side dish. Instead of being sharp and bitter, the onions were sweet, moist, and tender. I foresee this becoming a staple side dish in our family.

—Matt Morrison

My Mother's Coleslaw

I have never been able to make a really great summer salad, but my mom can throw vegetables, seasonings, and dressing in a bowl and make it all taste terrific. She prepared her coleslaw while I measured out each ingredient trying to balance all the flavors.

One time while she was making this slaw, she thought it was missing something sweet. She didn't want to add more sugar, so she tried some zucchini relish, but it wasn't quite right. She added some sweet pickle juice and that became the secret ingredient.

I don't like the creamy, mayonnaise-tasting coleslaw so often found in restaurants. This recipe is light on the mayo, and Mom presses her slaw to squeeze out the cabbage and carrot juices, which blends with the dressing, giving a more natural flavor to this dish.

12 sweet gherkins, finely grated, with $1/4$ cup of the pickle juice
5 medium carrots, grated coarsely
1 medium head cabbage, shredded
1 large sweet onion, finely grated
2 cups mayonnaise
$1/4$ cup sugar
$1/4$ cup apple cider vinegar
Salt and pepper

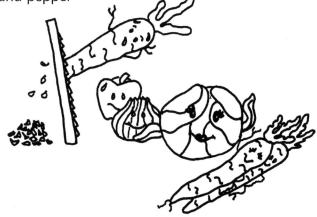

Optional:
   3 stalks celery, coarsely grated, or 1 tablespoon celery seed
   2 small purple-tip turnips, coarsely grated
   1 medium green pepper, coarsely grated

In a large bowl, mix all of the ingredients together, then pack into a deep container. Press frequently to extract the vegetable juices.

This coleslaw is better the next day.

Makes 8–10 servings

Cook's Tips

Use the shredder attachment of your food processor for the cabbage and carrots.

Use the blade of a food processor to finely chop the onion.

Omit the raw onion if it does not suit you.

I would like to emphasize the nice peppery taste that purple-tip turnips add.

While the flavors mingle overnight, use a potato masher to press the shredded cabbage as you would in making sauerkraut. This releases juices and enhances the coleslaw dressing.

Critics' Comments

This family slaw presents a brazen approach to a common American summer salad. Refreshing and less filling than traditional coleslaw, there is a distinctive sweet-onion flavoring with hints of a secret ingredient: sweet gherkin pickles.

—Peg and Marty Stout

Mom's Potato Salad

Everyone loves potato salad, macaroni salad, and coleslaw, but very few know how to make a great one of these salads. This is the recipe my mom makes, and I happen to think it's great!

    3 pounds white potatoes, peeled
    3 hard-cooked eggs, diced
    2 stalks celery, finely diced
    $1/2$ medium onion, finely diced
    $1/2$ green pepper, finely diced
    $3/4$ cup mayonnaise
    $1/4$ cup sour cream
    1 tablespoon mustard
    Salt and pepper
    1 hard-cooked egg, sliced (for garnish)
    Paprika (for garnish)

Boil the potatoes in salted water, drain and cool. Cut the potatoes into chunks.

Mix in the remaining ingredients. Adjust the seasonings to taste.

Garnish with the sliced egg and a sprinkling of paprika.

Makes 8–10 servings

Cook's Tips

Many people like red potatoes for a salad because they are waxy and hold their shape. I loathe potato salad made with red potatoes and their skins; their texture makes me feel like I'm chewing on paper.

I prefer a white chef's potato—it will mash a little for a creamier salad. Don't overcook the potatoes, or they will really mash.

You can use all mayonnaise, but adding the sour cream tames the mayonnaise flavor.

Finely dice the vegetables; you want their flavor, but not their presence.

Add more or less of the vegetables according to your taste.

Refrigerate the potatoes until cold after you boil them; they will hold their shape better.

Critics' Comments

A great accompaniment to a summer meal, this potato salad has a nice mixture of eggs, peppers, celery, and potato chunks. The subtle onion flavoring contributes to the tastiness, yet is not offensive to a non-onion lover! Mixed just lightly with mayonnaise, the potatoes and vegetables stand out as the dominant features of this salad.

—Peg and Marty Stout

Catalina Salad Dressing

This was the only salad dressing I would eat as a child; I loved the sweet and sour taste.

1 cup apple cider vinegar
1 cup sugar
$^1/_2$ teaspoon salt
1 large onion
1 can (10.5 ounces) tomato soup
1 cup olive oil
2–4 tablespoons sherry
2 cloves garlic

Bring the vinegar, sugar, and salt to a boil. Stir until the sugar is melted.

Puree the onion and add to the vinegar mixture. Stir in the tomato soup, then whisk in the olive oil. Finish with sherry to taste.

Pour the salad dressing into a clean wine bottle. Drop the garlic into the bottle and refrigerate for 24 hours.

Shake well before using.

Makes 1 quart

Cook's Tip

Experiment by adding, to the dressing bottle, various sprigs of fresh herbs, such as rosemary, oregano, basil, thyme, and parsley. Remove before serving.

Critic's Comments

This salad dressing reminded me of the original California dressing I've always loved. Aside from using it on a salad, it was a tangy treat as a dressing dip.

—Marilyn Prell

Mama's Green Tomato Pickle

My Dad grew plenty of tomatoes in his garden and always saved some green ones for Mama Sector to make her wonderful pickles.

2 cups salt
$1/2$ bushel green tomatoes, sliced
$1/2$ gallon apple cider vinegar
4 pounds brown sugar
1 ounce pickling spice
4 quarts onions, sliced
8 green bell peppers, sliced
8 red bell peppers, sliced

Sprinkle the salt over the green tomatoes and let sit at room temperature overnight. Cover with plastic wrap to contain a slightly unpleasant aroma. Drain thoroughly.

Make a brine by combining the apple cider vinegar and the brown sugar. Tie the pickling spice in cheesecloth and add to the brine; bring to a boil.

Add the onions and peppers and return to a boil.

Add the drained green tomatoes and return to a boil.

Pack into sterilized pint jars, seal, and turn upside down to cool.

Makes 8–10 pints

Cook's Tips

Some recipes recommend processing jars in a hot-water bath for 10 minutes.

Pickles may be stored at room temperature, but I like these pickles served chilled.

The red bell peppers add color and sweetness.

Strawberry Rhubarb Pudding Cake

My mom has always been involved in card groups: canasta, bridge, and cribbage. They take turns at each other's homes and the hostess serves dessert and coffee. I remember her canasta group always trying to outdo each other on desserts.

Mom has been a member of one bridge group for the past thirty years, and Mom, Helen, Jo, and Eila have shared life's experiences as they talk about children, husbands, jobs, and retirement and aging. These discussions have taken place over lunch, dessert, and card games, even a summer pajama party on Lake Winnipesaukee at Helen Walker's home, Breezy Island. This is Helen's recipe for Strawberry Rhubarb Pudding Cake.

1 quart rhubarb
2 cups strawberries
3 tablespoons salted butter
1^1/$_2$ cups cup sugar
^{1}/$_4$ cup water
1 cup milk
1 teaspoon vanilla
1 cup flour
2 teaspoons baking powder
^{1}/$_2$ teaspoon salt
^{1}/$_2$ teaspoon cinnamon
^{1}/$_4$ teaspoon nutmeg

For the topping:
1 tablespoon brown sugar
1 teaspoon granulated sugar
^{1}/$_4$ teaspoon cinnamon

Preheat the oven to 350°F.

Simmer the rhubarb, strawberries, 1 tablespoon of the butter, 1 cup of the sugar, and the water until the rhubarb is cooked and soft, about 10 minutes. Transfer to a 2-quart casserole dish.

Cream the remaining 2 tablespoons of the butter and the remaining $1/2$ cup of sugar until light and fluffy. Blend in the milk and vanilla. Stir in the flour, baking powder, salt, cinnamon and nutmeg. Pour the cake batter evenly over the strawberry-rhubarb mixture.

To make the topping, mix the sugars, and cinnamon and sprinkle over the cake. Bake for 30 minutes, or until a paring knife inserted into the center of the cake comes out clean.

Serve warm or at room temperature with ice cream, whipped cream, or powdered sugar.

Makes 5–6 servings

Cook's Tip

The original recipe calls for rhubarb only, but I like the addition of the strawberries.

Critics' Comments

A longstanding New England tradition of combining the sweetness of freshly picked strawberries with the tartness of rhubarb works well in this easy-to-make and always loved pudding cake. It's the perfect ending to an evening meal, a morning or afternoon treat with coffee or tea, or even lunch itself.

The strawberry-rhubarb combination is the top layer (when served) to a moist, tasty pudding cake.

—Peg and Marty Stout

Apple Dumplings

My mom made these dumplings with my sister and me, as children, after apple picking in the fall. I now make them with my students. I snicker over their attempts to work with pie dough, which for many students is their first time.

1 recipe for pie dough
4 baking apples, cored and peeled
3 tablespoon brown sugar
Vanilla
1/4 teaspoon cinnamon
dash nutmeg
1 teaspoon butter

Preheat the oven to 350°F.

Divide the pie dough into four equal parts. Roll each piece into a circle 1/8 inch thick.

Place an apple in the middle of each piece of the pie dough. Fill the center of each apple with brown sugar and two drops of vanilla. Sprinkle a little extra brown sugar around the apple. Dust each apple with cinnamon and nutmeg. Dot the center of the apple with a small piece of butter.

Bring the pie dough up around the apple, wrapping it tightly. Place the apples in a 9-inch square baking pan.

For the sauce:
$1^1/_2$ cups water
$2/_3$ cup brown sugar
$1/_4$ teaspoon cinnamon

Bring the water, brown sugar, and cinnamon to a boil, then pour around the apples. Bake the apples for 45 to 55 minutes, or until the apples are soft and the crust is golden brown. Serve the dumplings with a little bit of the sauce drizzled on top.

Makes 4 servings

Cook's Tips

I like Cortland apples for baking, but granny smiths, Macintosh, Baldwin, and Rome beauty apples are nice substitutes.

Ready-made pie dough can be used successfully.

The sauce definitely makes these dumplings; don't omit it.

Critic's Comments

Yet another sinful dessert! These dumplings are incredible! The crust is both crispy and moist, and the apples are sweet and tart. Save room for these. They're big, and you'll savor every bite.

—Matt Morrison

Sour Cherry Nut Cake

My aunt Francis gave this recipe to Mom. The recipe is dated 1947. This cake has been served at many baby and wedding showers in my family, and it always disappears fast.

$1/3$ cup salted butter
$1^1/2$ cups sugar
2 eggs
$1/2$ teaspoon vanilla
$2^1/2$ cups flour
$1^1/2$ teaspoons baking powder
$1/2$ teaspoon baking soda
$1/2$ teaspoon salt
1 cup whole milk
1 can sour cherries, drained
$1/2$ cup walnuts, chopped
Sweetened whipped cream

Preheat the oven to 350°F.

Cream the butter and sugar. Beat in the eggs and vanilla.

Sift together the flour, baking powder, baking soda, and salt. Add to the creamed mixture alternately with the milk.

Fold in the sour cherries and nuts.

Pour the batter into a greased and floured 9x13-inch cake pan. Bake for 50 to 55 minutes, or until a paring knife inserted into the center of the cake comes out clean. Let the cake sit in the pan for 15 minutes before unmolding. Cool to room temperature.

To serve, spread sweetened whipped cream over the top of the cake.

Makes 12 servings

Cook's Tips

Whipped cream definitely makes this cake; don't omit it.

Substitute pecans for the walnuts.

Substitute almond extract for the vanilla.

Critic's Comments

Not only is this the best dessert of Joan's I have ever experienced (and that is certainly saying a lot), but this is also the best dessert I have ever had. Like most superb things, this dessert is nearly impossible to describe. All I can say is that the cake is moist, the cherries tart, and the walnuts sweet. Relax and take time to truly *experience* this dessert.

—Matt Morrison

Mama's Hot Milk Sponge Cake

While in college, I frequently stopped by to visit with Mama and Papa Sector. Mama always had homemade pastry to go with a good cup of coffee and her Hot Milk Sponge Cake was a favorite of mine. Mama and I would sit for hours on her porch, conversing about our lives. I fondly remember those times and cherish her loving advice.

Cake
2 eggs
1 cup sugar
1 cup flour
1 teaspoon baking powder
$1/2$ teaspoon salt
$1/2$ cup hot milk
2 tablespoons butter
1 teaspoon vanilla

Topping
3 tablespoons butter
$3/4$ cup brown sugar
3 tablespoons heavy cream
1 cup shredded coconut
1 cup chopped pecans
$1/2$ teaspoon vanilla

Preheat the oven to 375°F.

In a large mixing bowl, beat the eggs until very thick and light. Add the sugar and beat very, very well.

In a separate bowl, sift the flour, baking powder, and salt.

Melt the butter in the hot milk and add the vanilla.

Add the flour mixture and the hot milk to the beaten eggs all at once and fold in quickly. Pour the batter into an ungreased 9-inch square cake pan. Bake for 30 minutes, or until a paring knife inserted into the center of the cake comes out clean. Let the cake stand a few minutes on a cooling rack.

For the topping, melt the butter over low heat, then add the brown sugar, and the cream. Stir in the coconut and nuts.

Spread the coconut mixture over the cake. Return it to the oven and broil until the top is brown and bubbly, 2 to 3 minutes. Serve at room temperature.

Makes 9 servings

Cook's Tips

Use a mixer with a wire whip to make the batter. Set it to high power to beat the eggs and sugar; use low power to fold in the flour and milk.

The best nuts for this recipe are pecans, but walnuts, pistachios, and filberts can be used.

Do not grease the cake pan; a sponge cake will not rise.

Critic's Comments

With the first bite, the sponge just melts in your mouth; with the second bite, the crunchy sweetness of the topping bursts into your mouth! You can't eat just one piece!

—Marilyn Prell

Holiday Cake

My mom made these cakes frequently during the Christmas holidays. She wrapped them in colored aluminum foil and gave them as gifts, a tradition I have continued throughout the years.

1/2 cup pecans, finely chopped
8 ounces cream cheese, softened to room temperature
2 sticks salted butter, softened to room temperature
1 1/2 cups sugar
1 1/2 teaspoons vanilla
4 eggs
2 1/4 cups cake flour
1 1/2 teaspoons baking powder
1/4 teaspoon cinnamon
3/4 cup drained maraschino cherries, chopped
1/2 cup pecans, chopped

For the glaze
1 1/2 cups confectioner's sugar
2 tablespoons milk
A drop of vanilla

For garnish
Maraschino cherry halves
Pecan halves

Preheat the oven to 325°F.

Grease a tube or bundt pan with butter and dust with the finely chopped pecans. Set aside.

Beat together the cream cheese, butter, sugar, and vanilla until light and smooth.

Add the eggs, one at a time, mixing well after each addition.

Add the flour, baking powder, cinnamon, cherries, and chopped pecans and blend just until ingredients come together.

Pour the batter into the prepared pan and bake for $1^1/_4$ to $1^1/_2$ hours, or until a paring knife inserted into the center of the cake comes out clean. Cool for 5 minutes, then remove from the pan.

To glaze the cake, blend the sugar, milk and vanilla. Drizzle over the top and sides of the cake.

Decorate with the cherry halves and the pecan halves.

Makes 10–12 servings

Cook's Tip

I sometimes bake this cake in a clean coffee can. Unmold, decorate, and enfold in plastic wrap for a holiday gift.

Substitute almonds or walnuts for the pecans.

If using almonds, substitute almond extract for the vanilla.

Critic's Comments

This wonderful cake brings together a delicious blend of nuts and berries to make the perfect dessert or late-night winter snack with a cup of tea. Along with a hint of cinnamon, the maraschino cherry flavor dominates this cake but never overpowers it, while the walnuts take the edge off the natural sweetness of the fruit. The sugary glaze adds just the right touch of "dessert" to the mix, making this a recipe for all occasions, whether it's coffee and cake with friends, dessert with the family, or your contribution to a potluck party.

—Scott Strainge

CHAPTER THREE

My Cooking Passion

≋ My Cooking Passion

While I was probably born with a predisposition for loving food and cooking, my first acknowledgment of this passion was at age ten, when my cousins Sandy and Sue Styrna gave me my first cookbook for Christmas: a Betty Crocker cookbook that entertained me for years. Every Saturday I made lunch for my family and used this cookbook as my guide. I continued collecting Betty Crocker cookbooks for many years and had fun experimenting with the recipes, making changes to suit my whims. The recipes were easy and enabled me to be creative.

When I was a junior in high school, a little restaurant opened up in town called the Eagle's Nest. I walked there after school and worked as a waitress through the evening hours. Even though I was learning the dining room operations, my interests were in the kitchen. Mary, the cook, was a big woman, serious, demanding, and ornery. Although a bit afraid of her, I was intrigued watching Mary cook and maneuver about this little kitchen.

Mary made wonderful grape-nut custard. I carried a spoon in my pocket and when the occasion came for me to go into the kitchen refrigerator, I quickly enjoyed a mouthful or two. Mary started complaining about how often she had to make grape-nut custard, and though she eventually figured out what was happening, by then I had won her heart and she whispered in my ear every time she made grape-nut custard.

While waitressing at the Eagle's Nest, I took an interest in food with my mom. On snowy days off from school, she and I sat at the dining room table, still in our pajamas, browsing through cookbooks looking for recipes to experiment with. We sat there until after noon, enjoying this common interest.

As my sister, Christine, and I were approaching our college years, Mom went to work to help pay the expenses. Our job was to have dinner ready when Mom and Dad got home. Chris didn't care for cooking, but I lovingly accepted the challenge. I planned the menus using Mom's collection of cookbooks and had dinner waiting every night. I looked forward to the family's critiques and compliments.

When college began, I took a job in the kitchen at the Old Mill in Westminster, Massachusetts. This was a well-known and very busy restaurant serving breakfast, lunch, and dinner seven days a week, year-round. My family had celebrated many special occasions here, so I was excited when I was offered the job. The Old Mill restaurant is still operating today. I worked days, weekends, holidays, and summer vacations for three years, and consider this the foundation of my cooking skills. I began with basic preparations, learning knife skills and kitchen procedures. I was trained to cook a full breakfast. I made salads and platters for a salad bar. During lunch, I fired off the hot meals as I learned how to broil, grill, roast, and deep-fry.

I quickly got to know the chefs, who shared their knowledge and talents with me. As I gained more experience, the chefs allowed me to prepare dishes for catered events and evening buffets. I learned about the attractiveness of food presentation and garnishing. This "work" was actually real fun!

Breakfast at the Old Mill was a popular event on weekends. Since I was its breakfast cook, I perfected the art of preparing eggs. On my first Easter Sunday at the restaurant, I was given two assistants to help with side dishes and garnishing. They never showed up! The chefs were busy preparing for Easter dinner, so I was on my own except for brief moments when a chef could assist. The manager stood by watching, providing praise and encouragement. I think he was also praying! Later that day, the manager announced that I had prepared approximately six hundred meals in three hours. Everyone around me was amazed with my performance, including me.

I wisely chose a major of home economics in college so that cooking good food could continue to be not only a hobby, but a possible career as well. During this time I was learning all I could about the art of cooking and soliciting recipes from my professors, employers, coworkers, family, and friends. I also started collecting the Time-Life series of American and international cookbooks. These are out of print now, but I still refer to the recipes. Because my parents entertained frequently, I would often choose a country from these cookbooks or put together new recipes I had acquired; I would

plan, prepare, and serve a meal to their guests. Everyone loved dinner at our house, and I loved doing the cooking.

Some of my favorite recipes as a child through my college years are included in the following sampling.

Hamburg Noodle Bake Casserole

I served Hamburg Noodle Bake Casserole to a friend who loved it so much that he wrote a song about it. Every time I make this dish, I find myself singing the song!

8 ounces cream cheese, softened
1/4 cup evaporated milk
1/2 teaspoon fresh lemon juice
1/4 teaspoon fresh minced garlic
1/4 teaspoon salt
6 cups egg noodles, cooked
1 medium green pepper, diced
1 medium onion, diced
1 pound hamburger
1 can (8ounces) tomato sauce
1/4 cup ketchup

Preheat the oven to 350°F.

Combine the cream cheese, evaporated milk, lemon juice, garlic, and salt. Mix with the hot noodles, then transfer to a buttered 3-quart casserole.

Sauté the green pepper and onion until soft. Add the hamburger and brown well. Add the tomato sauce and ketchup. Pour over the noodles.

Bake for 25 to 30 minutes, or until the cheese and tomato sauces are bubbling.

Makes 4 servings

Cook's Tips

I like the medium wide egg noodles in this recipe, but you can choose your favorites.

For a richer texture, substitute marscapone cheese for the cream cheese and cream for the evaporated milk.

Add some herbs to the tomato sauce such as oregano, basil or Italian seasoning.

I love garlic and have a tendency to use a bit more than the recipe calls for.

Critic's Comments

What make this recipe so great are the surprise ingredients and the wonderfully delicious tastes they create. I love the interaction among the moist noodles, the cream cheese, and the hamburger; somehow they create a sweet and tangy flavor that's addicting. I'm a huge lasagna fan, but I think this dish outdoes even that long time favorite.

—Matt Morrison

Chinese Pepper Steak

May Huang was my college professor and mentor. She was born and raised in Canton, China, and educated in the United States. One evening May invited my college roommate Aletha and me to her apartment for dinner. She asked us what we would like and we requested a Chinese meal typical of her homeland. She prepared pepper steak and braised soy sauce beef. I still have May's original recipes, which she mimeographed for us. May served us a wonderful meal, which I continue to make today.

1 pound flank steak
2 medium green peppers
3 tablespoons soy sauce
1 tablespoon dry sherry
2 teaspoons cornstarch
1 teaspoon sugar
1/4 cup peanut oil
4 slices fresh gingerroot, 1/8 inch thick, cut into fine dice

Cut the steak crosswise into 1/4 inch slices, then lengthwise into 1 1/2 inch strips.

Remove the seeds and stems from the green peppers. Cut into 1/2 inch squares.

Mix together sherry, the soy sauce, cornstarch, and sugar. Add the steak and stir to coat. Let marinate for 4 to 6 hours.

Heat 2 tablespoons of the oil in a sauté pan over high heat. When the oil begins to smoke, add the green

pepper and stir-fry until tender but still crisp. Remove from the pan and set aside.

Add the remaining 2 tablespoons of oil to the pan and heat on high. When the oil begins to smoke, add the ginger and the steak mixture and stir-fry until the meat shows no sign of pink.

Return the green peppers to the sauté pan and stir-fry until heated through. Serve over rice.

Makes 4 servings

Cook's Tips

I prefer tenderloin steak for this recipe, but flank is quite acceptable and less pricey.

Replace the green peppers with snow peas or broccoli, but parboil the broccoli first to make it tender.

Critic's Comments

I'm fanatical about steak. This is not to say that I love the meat, but I am indeed fanatical about the way that steak is prepared. I've never been someone who can eat a blank steak: I need spices—food is merely a vehicle for sauce, powder, drizzle, and glaze. So the preparation of the steak is of great importance to me, and I can safely say that this steak recipe will not let down all my fellow fans of flavor. I enjoyed the meal for dinner on a bed of rice. The steak was tenderized by the marinade and complemented by the starchy rice accompaniment. I've never been a proponent of cooked vegetables, but the cooked peppers added to the flavor of the steak and completed a hearty and satisfying meal. Just the right amount of flavor brings this Asian dish to life.

—Brian Deveney

Braised Soy Sauce Beef

May Huang, my college professor, prepared this dish along with Chinese pepper steak for dinner one evening, for my college room-mate and me.

2 pounds lean boneless chuck
1^1/$_2$ cups water
^{1}/$_4$ cup dry sherry
^{1}/$_4$ cup soy sauce
4 cloves of garlic, minced
4 whole star anise
4 scallions cut into 1-inch lengths
2 large onions, diced
2 slices gingerroot, ^{1}/$_8$ inch thick, diced
2 teaspoon Szechwan pepper, crushed
1 teaspoon crushed red pepper
1 teaspoon sugar
^{1}/$_2$ teaspoon salt
3 tablespoons peanut oil

Trim the fat from the beef and cut into 1^1/$_2$ inch cubes and set aside. In a large mixing bowl, combine the other ingredients except the peanut oil and set aside.

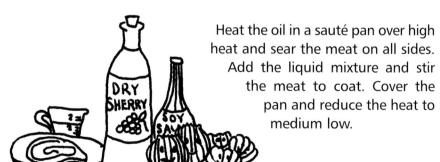

Heat the oil in a sauté pan over high heat and sear the meat on all sides. Add the liquid mixture and stir the meat to coat. Cover the pan and reduce the heat to medium low.

Simmer slowly until the meat is tender, $1^1/_2$ to 2 hours. Stir occasionally to prevent the meat from sticking to the pan. The liquid will reduce to about $^1/_2$ cup of rich sauce.

Serve with boiled rice.

Makes 4–6 servings

Cook's Tip

This recipe is moderately spicy. The amounts of Szechwan and crushed red pepper can be adjusted according to your heat index.

Spanish Rice

As a child, I made Spanish Rice for my family for lunch almost every Saturday. I had fun experimenting with a variety of spices.

1 green pepper, diced
1 large onion, diced
2 tablespoons olive oil
1 pound ground beef
1 cup rice, uncooked
2 teaspoons Cajun seasoning
1 teaspoon chili powder
1 teaspoon Mexican seasoning
1 teaspoon oregano
1 teaspoon salt
1/2 teaspoon pepper
3 1/2 cups water
1 cup tomato sauce
1/4 cup barbecue sauce
2 tablespoons ketchup

Sauté the green pepper and onion in olive oil until the onions are translucent.

Add the ground beef and sauté until the meat falls apart, breaking it up as it cooks.

Add the rice, Cajun seasoning, chili powder, Mexican seasoning, oregano, salt and pepper; sauté about 5 minutes.

Add the water, tomato sauce, barbecue sauce, and ketchup. Cover and simmer for 20 to 25 minutes, until the rice is cooked and soft.

Cook's Tip

Increase the heat by adding a few splashes of your favorite hot sauce.

Mrs. Foster's Broccoli Salad

Down the street from where I lived as a child was a big, white, beautifully maintained farmhouse. The owners, Mr. and Mrs. Foster, gave me various jobs from the time I was in the sixth grade through college. Mr. Foster's brother owned the Old Mill restaurant, where I worked during college. Because of these opportunities to work and my parents' generosity, I had no college debt when I graduated.

I began by weeding gardens at the farm, filling the water tank for the cows, and doing light housekeeping. As I grew older, the Fosters gave me more responsibility. During college, I was cooking some meals for the Foster family, and when they entertained I prepared many of the dishes.

This was when I started baking homemade yeast breads with frequent success. Mr. Foster loved cheese bread and I experimented with various cheeses until I got a combination I liked. Today I make this bread just to have French toast. What a treat!

Mrs. Foster, a graduate of Skidmore College in home economics, was my idol and role model. An immaculate, organized, gracious, and feminine woman, she had my greatest admiration and I wanted to be just like her. It was important to me to have her acceptance, and I always did. As a teacher, I have been told that I have affected more lives than I will ever know. Mrs. Foster affected my life more than she will ever know.

1 large bunch broccoli crowns
3 hard-cooked eggs, chopped
1 cup chopped celery
1 cup mayonnaise
$1/2$ cup sliced green olives, with pimento
$1/2$ cup diced onion
1 tablespoon fresh lemon juice

Blanch the broccoli in boiling water for 30 seconds, then let cool. Chop into $1/2$ inch pieces.

Add the remaining ingredients and blend well. Chill until ready to serve.

Makes 4 servings

Cook's Tips

This recipe is best made a day ahead.

Blanching the broccoli brings out its bright green color without cooking it. Do not cover the pot while blanching.

Use an egg slicer to chop the eggs; turn the eggs in the opposite direction to get a cross-cut.

Garnish with bleu cheese for extra flavor.

Critics Comments

This dish was such a pleasant surprise. Having never heard of anything like it, I wasn't sure what to expect, but after devouring far too much of it, I was convinced. This salad is out-of-this world good and is the perfect complement to any meal.

—Matt Morrison

Ritz Cracker Stuffing

The Old Mill restaurant made the best Ritz cracker stuffing for its baked stuffed shrimp and lobster. I secured the list of ingredients, but not the proportions. This recipe is what I recollect.

1^1/$_2$ cups bread crumbs
1^1/$_2$ cups Ritz cracker crumbs
6–8 tablespoons butter, melted
3 tablespoons lemon juice
1^1/$_2$ teaspoons garlic salt
1 teaspoon paprika
^{1}/$_2$ teaspoon pepper

Combine all the ingredients. Add enough butter to bind the stuffing together.

Makes 3 cups

Cook's Tips

Make bread crumbs and cracker crumbs using a food processor.

Use this stuffing mix for seafood dishes, such as baked stuffed haddock and baked stuffed shrimp.

Drizzle a little more melted butter on the stuffing just before it goes into the oven.

Sally Dyer's Pickles

While I was in college, Sally Dyer, the home economics teacher at the middle school in my hometown, invited me into her classroom. I observed her teaching and occasionally taught small lessons. I am grateful to Sally for making my early experiences in the classroom unintimidating and guiding me into a lifelong profession.

Sally's recipe for pickles is different and absolutely delicious.

2 quarts cucumbers	$1/4$ cup flour
2 large onions	$1^1/_2$ teaspoons celery seed
3 tablespoons coarse salt	$1^1/_2$ teaspoons mustard seed
1 quart water	$1/_2$ teaspoon turmeric
$1^1/_2$ cups sugar	2 cups cider vinegar

Peel and cut the cucumbers into 1-inch cubes.

Slice onions and combine with cucumbers. Add salt and cover with the water; let stand for 3 hours. Drain and rinse with cold water. Set aside.

In a large pot, combine dry ingredients along with the vinegar and cook over medium-high heat, stirring constantly, until you have a boil. Add the cucumbers and onions and stir until they heat through.

Can the pickles according to the manufacturer's directions for your canning equipment.

Makes 6 pints

Cook's Tip

Do not double this recipe; it never seems to thicken properly.

Eggnog

Professor Margaret Chickering taught foods and nutrition at Keene State College in New Hampshire. I took several of her courses. I found her recipes for Eggnog, Hot Fruited Tea and Hot Mulled Cider to be exceptional.

6 egg whites
$3/4$ cup sugar
6 egg yolks
$1/8$ teaspoon salt
4 cups milk
1 teaspoon vanilla
Nutmeg, for garnish

Beat the egg whites until stiff. Beat in $1/4$ cup of the sugar and set aside.

In another bowl, beat the yolks, the remaining $1/2$ cup of sugar, and the salt until very light and airy.

Combine the egg mixtures and stir until thoroughly blended. Add the milk and vanilla. Garnish with a dusting of nutmeg.

Makes 5 cups

Hot Fruited Tea

5 cups boiling water
5 tea bags
10 whole cloves
$1/4$ teaspoon cinnamon
$1/2$ cup sugar
$1/2$ cup fresh lemon juice
$1/3$ cup fresh orange juice

Pour the boiling water over the tea bags. Add the cloves and cinnamon. Cover and steep for 5 minutes; strain tea. Add the sugar and citrus juices. Heat to just below boiling.

Makes 5 cups

Hot Mulled Cider

2 quarts cider
$1/2$ cup brown sugar
1 cinnamon stick, 3 inches long
1 teaspoon whole cloves
$1/4$ teaspoon salt
8 orange slices, for garnish

Combine all of the ingredients and slowly bring to a boil. Simmer, covered, for 20 minutes. Remove the cinnamon stick and cloves.

Serve hot, garnished with the orange slices.

Makes 8 cups

Cranberry Goodin' Puddin'

From Professor Margaret Chickering

1 cup cranberries
3/4 cup sugar
1/4 cup chopped walnuts
1 egg
1/2 cup flour
6 tablespoon butter, melted
Vanilla ice cream, to serve

Preheat the oven to 325°F.

Butter a 9-inch pie pan. Spread the cranberries over the bottom and sprinkle with 1/4 cup of the sugar and the walnuts.

In a small mixing bowl, beat the egg. Gradually add 1/2 cup of the sugar as you beat. Add the flour and melted butter to the egg mixture, beating well to incorporate.

Pour the batter over the cranberries, then bake for 45 minutes, or until the crust is golden brown. Cut as you would a pie and serve warm with vanilla ice cream.

Makes 8 servings

Cook's Tip

Substitute pecans, almonds and pistachios for the walnuts.

Critic's Comments

Like all of Joan's desserts, this one is perfect. If you love cranberries and walnuts, this dessert is definitely for you. With the sweet on the bottom and the tart on top, you really can't help but dig in for more after every bite.

—Matt Morrison

Mary's Grape-Nut Custard

Mary, the cook at the Eagle's Nest restaurant, shared this recipe with me.

$^3/_4$ cup boiling water
$^1/_2$ cup grape nuts
2 eggs
2 egg yolks
$^1/_2$ cup sugar
2 cups milk
1 teaspoon vanilla
1 tablespoon butter
Whipped cream, for garnish

Preheat the oven to 350°F.

Pour the boiling water over the grape nuts and set aside.

Whisk together the eggs, yolks, and sugar.

Scald the milk and whisk into the egg mixture. Add the grape nuts and vanilla.

Butter a 1$^1/_2$-quart baking dish. Pour the custard into the dish and dot with butter. Bake in a hot-water bath for 1 hour, or until a paring knife inserted into the center of the custard comes out clean.

Serve cold with a dollop of whipped cream.

Makes 4–6 servings

Cook's Tips

The gentle cooking in a hot-water bath makes this pudding so silken.

To bake in a hot-water bath, place the custard dish in a large, shallow pan of hot water that comes halfway up the side of the dish.

Critic's Comments

This pudding's texture was silken! It even tasted smooth, all flavors blending deliciously. Be careful you don't eat the whole pudding!

—Marilyn Prell

Caramel Popcorn Balls

Caramel popcorn balls are an impressive Christmas decoration and a great treat for children. My mom made popcorn balls with my sister and me every Christmas. We wrapped them in plastic wrap, tied them with red ribbons, attached candy canes to them, and hung them on the tree. On Christmas Day we gathered these popcorn ball decorations and gave them to my cousins as gifts, saving some for ourselves, of course!

All who know her appreciate my mom's creative efforts at Christmas. I remember fondly how she decorated the fireplace mantel with evergreens from the backyard, huge popcorn balls, and big candy canes. One year when she was working at the local middle school, a group of student carolers came to our home. Fifty children filled the living room and sang, much to the delight of my parents. Mom gave a decorated popcorn ball to each child. That was Christmas from her heart and a great tradition over the years.

4–5 quarts popped corn
$^1/_2$ teaspoon salt
1 tablespoon butter
1 cup molasses
$^1/_2$ cup sugar

Pick over the popped corn, discard any unpopped kernels, and sprinkle with the salt. Set aside.

Melt the butter. Add the sugar and molasses. Bring to a boil, then reduce the heat to medium and cook for 5 minutes. The sugar should come to the brittle stage, 270°F.

Pour this mixture over the popped popcorn and with a rubber spatula, quickly stir the popcorn around until it is coated with the sugar mixture.

Butter your hands and gently press the popcorn into balls, the size of a baseball. Wrap each separately in plastic wrap, twisting the tops to close.

Makes about 18 popcorn balls

Cook's Tips

$1/2$ cup popcorn kernels will yield about $1^1/2$ quarts, popped.

To test for the brittle stage in candy making, drop a little hot sugar mixture into a glass of ice-cold water. The sugar should form a hard, sticky mass.

Be very careful when stirring the sugar mixture into the popcorn. It is very hot and could cause a serious burn.

Buttering your hands when forming the popcorn balls prevents them from sticking to your hands. Butter again after every other one.

Critic's Comments

This light and airy treat is just the thing for a snack, for holiday decoration, or for munching around the house anytime. Unlike the store-bought brand, these delectable edibles are not covered with a hard sugary crust. Instead, the caramel acts like a glue for the popcorn, nestling itself in the nooks and crannies and giving it shape along with a great caramel taste that accents the popcorn flavor. Make a batch, send them to school with the kids for parties, decorate for the holidays, or put them out for a summer barbecue treat. They will be sure to please for all occasions!

—Scott Strainge

Apple Crisp

1/4 cup water
1 teaspoon cinnamon
1/4 teaspoon nutmeg
1/2 teaspoon salt
4 cups sliced apples
1 cup sugar
3/4 cup flour
6 tablespoons butter
Ice cream, to serve

Preheat the oven to 375°F.

Combine the water, cinnamon, nutmeg and salt in a large mixing bowl. Add the apple slices and toss to coat. Transfer to an ungreased 9-inch baking pan.

Put the sugar, flour, and butter into a food processor with the blade and pulse until the mixture looks like fine crumbs. Do not over process or a paste will form. Spread over the apples.

Bake uncovered, for 1 hour, or until the topping is golden brown. Serve at room temperature with ice cream.

Cook's Tip

I like Cortland apples for baking, but granny smiths, Macintosh, Baldwin and Rome beauty are nice substitutes.

Critic's Comments

This apple crisp is a delightfully sweet and tender traditional dessert. The blend of Cortland apples and spices makes for a delectable treat. Unlike many others, this recipe gives the "crisp" a very smooth and pleasing texture. To enhance the dish even further, consider drizzling lightly with a caramel sauce and vanilla bean ice cream. Certainly this accompaniment is not necessary, as the dessert is a stand-alone winner for children and adults alike.

—Jenifer Pellerin

Peanut Butter-Cornflake Cookies

The cafeteria's in my elementary, middle, and high school frequently made these cookies. The kids would return to the kitchen after lunch to buy the extras. My mom was able to secure this recipe when she worked at the middle school as a secretary, so I am able to make this fondly remembered childhood treat.

1 1/2 cups sugar
3/4 cup Karo corn syrup
1 cup peanut butter
6 cups cornflakes

Combine the sugar and Karo syrup and cook in a medium saucepan over medium-high heat until the sugar is dissolved and the mixture is clear, 4–5 minutes.

Remove from the heat and stir in the peanut butter. Pour this mixture over the cornflakes and mix well. Spread evenly in a well-buttered 9-inch square cake pan. Cut into bars while still warm; cool before serving.

Makes 9 cookies

Cook's Tips

Do not overcook the sugar and Karo or the cookies will be rock solid.

Work quickly when stirring the peanut butter mixture into the cornflakes. As the mixture cools, it firms up.

Basically, this is peanut butter fudge with cornflakes mixed in to provide a crunch.

Critic's Comments

These truly melt in your mouth, with an added crunch!

—Marilyn Prell

Chocolate Chip Cookies

This is a favorite recipe and easy for children to make.

1^1/$_2$ sticks salted butter
^{1}/$_2$ cup brown sugar, packed
^{1}/$_2$ cup granulated sugar
2 eggs
1 teaspoon vanilla
2 cups flour
1 teaspoon baking soda
1 cup chocolate chips

Preheat the oven to 350°F.

Cream together the butter and sugars. Beat in the eggs and vanilla. Blend in the remaining ingredients.

Using a small ice-cream scoop, scoop out the dough onto an ungreased sheet pan. Bake for 10 to 12 minutes, or until light golden brown.

Makes 12 cookies

Cook's Tips

Use good-quality chocolate from a candy store and chop into pieces.

Dark, milk, and white chocolate will all work well.

For a variation, replace the chocolate chips with M&M's. Set three or four M&M's into the top of each cookie before they go into the oven.

Try white chocolate with macadamia nuts for another variation.

Be creative with the kinds of candies and nuts used in place of the chocolate chips.

Peanut Blossoms

1 stick salted butter
$^1/_2$ cup brown sugar, packed
$^1/_2$ cup granulated sugar, plus more for rolling
$^1/_2$ cup peanut butter
1 egg
2 tablespoon milk
1 teaspoon vanilla
$1^3/_4$ cups flour
1 teaspoon baking soda
$^1/_2$ teaspoon salt
Walnut halves, optional

Preheat the oven to 375°F.

Cream the butter, the brown sugar, and $^1/_2$ cup of the granulated sugar until light and fluffy.

Beat in the peanut butter, egg, milk, and vanilla.

Blend in the flour, baking soda, and salt. Shape the dough into small balls the size of walnuts. Roll the balls in sugar and place them on an ungreased sheet pan. Top each cookie with a walnut half and bake for 12 to 15 minutes, or until light golden brown. Do not over bake.

Makes 18 cookies

Cook's Tip

Top each cookie with a Hershey's kiss before baking.

Critic's Comments

Admittedly, when I decided to try these cookies, I wasn't convinced I would enjoy them. The thought of peanut and walnut intermingling on my taste buds worried me. However, upon tasting, all my concerns dissipated. The moist, buttery cookies melted in my mouth. The walnuts complement the flavor of the peanut butter very well. Do not alter this aspect of the recipe, for it ensures that these peanut butter cookies will be far superior to any other! The texture and flavor meld seamlessly into a wonderful snack or dessert, especially if served with a tall glass of cold milk.

—Jenifer Pellerin

Mrs. Foster's Gingersnaps

I'm not fond of gingersnaps, but these are fabulous!

1 cup sugar, plus extra for dipping
$^3/_4$ cup shortening
$^1/_4$ cup molasses
1 egg
2 cups flour
1 teaspoon baking powder
1 teaspoon baking soda
1 teaspoon cinnamon
1 teaspoon cloves
1 teaspoon ginger

Preheat the oven to 350°F.

Cream the sugar and the shortening until light and fluffy.

Beat in the molasses and egg.

Stir in the dry ingredients.

Roll into small balls. Dip in the extra sugar.

Place on a greased cookie sheet. Press the top of each with a fork. Bake for 8 to 10 minutes, or until lightly golden brown.

Makes 24 cookies

Critic's Comments

These were softly moist yet firm, instead of the usual dry and crisp types. There was no harsh ginger "afterbite." We liked them even better than gingerbread.

—Marilyn Prell

$\mathcal{B}$utterscotch $\mathcal{B}$rownies

$^1/_2$ stick salted butter
1 cup brown sugar, packed
1 egg
$^3/_4$ cup flour
$^1/_2$ cup chopped walnuts, optional
1 teaspoon baking powder
$^1/_2$ teaspoon salt
$^1/_2$ teaspoon vanilla

Preheat the oven to 350ºF.

Melt the butter over low heat. Remove from the heat and stir in the brown sugar; let cool.

Stir in the egg. Add the remaining ingredients and blend well. Spread into a greased and floured 8-inch baking pan. Bake for 30 to 35 minutes, or until lightly golden brown. Do not over bake. Cool in the pan, then cut into squares.

Makes 9 brownies

Molasses Crinkles

My mom's specialties were cookies, spice cakes, and custards. Molasses is a choice ingredient in her kitchen, and in mine, too.

1^1/$_2$ sticks salted butter, softened
1 cup brown sugar, packed
1 egg
^{1}/$_4$ cup molasses
2^1/$_4$ cups flour
2 teaspoons baking soda
1 teaspoon cinnamon
1 teaspoon ginger
^{1}/$_2$ teaspoon cloves
^{1}/$_4$ teaspoon salt

In a large mixing bowl, cream the butter and brown sugar. Beat in the egg and molasses.

Blend in the remaining ingredients. Chill the dough for one hour or until it becomes firm.

Preheat the oven to 375°F.

Roll the dough into balls the size of walnuts. Dip the tops in sugar and place sugar-side up on a sheet pan. Mist the cookies with water for a crackled surface. Bake for 10 to 12 minutes, until set but not hard.

Makes 24 cookies

CHAPTER FOUR

Apprenticing in San Francisco

Apprenticing in San Francisco

My first job out of college was teaching cooking at Gallagher Junior High in Leominster, Massachusetts. During the day I worked intensely to get 150 seventh- and eighth-grade students to develop basic cooking skills and a love for the process of creating good, healthy foods. In the evening I worked to refine my own skills by taking classes at Modern Gourmet Boston, Madeleine Kamman's cooking school in Newton Centre. I studied there for two years, learning a tremendous amount from Kamman's former students, who operated a renowned restaurant on the premises and taught the workshops. It was there that my skills in cooking moved from basic/adequate to more refined and specialized.

In 1980, the state of Massachusetts passed Proposition $2^1/_2$, which limits the amount of property taxes a town or city can collect. This resulted in major cutbacks in education and hundreds of teachers were laid off. My days at Gallagher Junior High ended and I joined the unemployment lines.

As I was deciding what to do next, my landlord, Helen Willard, came across an article about a chef's training program at the San Francisco Culinary Academy. The article piqued my interest, so I applied and was accepted.

With the help of friends, I found an apartment in the San Jose area, and rode the public transit into San Francisco for classes at the academy. The change from my East Coast life was exciting; California cooking seemed different, and I was ready to learn all there was to know about it. After spending the first semester at the academy, however, I realized that I had learned so much more at Modern Gourmet Boston. The mysteries of California cooking were not mysteries at all; I was ready to end classes and put what I knew as a chef into action.

While searching the local papers for cooking opportunities, I found an ad for a prep cook at the executive dining room for the computer company Atari. I contacted its executive chef, Anton Dietz, for an interview and immediately felt a good rapport with Tony. He offered me the job and I began two weeks later.

My responsibilities included creating appetizers and salads. Tony recognized my vast knowledge of food and cooking, but as a former chef/instructor at the San Francisco Culinary Academy, he also realized that I was still lacking some important skills. He patiently taught me what I needed to do to be successful. I quickly learned professional knife skills and gained confidence in handling large knives. I learned the full meaning behind the French phrase mise en place, which means having all the ingredients necessary for a dish prepared and ready to combine up to the point of cooking. I learned the art of homemade stocks and practiced making a variety of sauces from those stocks. I joined Tony in planning the menus and daily specials, and he guided me in ordering and receiving foodstuffs for the dining room. Because each meal was prepared to order, I was introduced to the sauté station. I thrived in this learning environment and eventually the responsibility of the kitchen was handed to me.

As the sous-chef for the executive dining room at Atari, my day began at six in the morning placing orders to food vendors. I got the soup ready for simmering, prepared bread dough for rising, butchered meats, trimmed fish and chicken, blanched vegetables, made rice pilaf, and baked dozens of oatmeal and chocolate chip cookies for the day.

The cookies I baked seemed to be appreciated by all, so I made dozens of them for the dining room every morning, but wondered why some seemed mysteriously to disappear. One night when I stayed later than usual, I saw the waiters with a silver tray piled high with cookies and handing them out to the corporate secretaries. I snickered when I figured out that the waiters were flirting with my cookies!

As a young female sous-chef for the impressive corporate offices of Atari, I encountered many good-looking executives daily. I had to wear a chef's uniform but wanted to look my best, so I dolled up my hair and put on makeup and lipstick every morning. One day, as lunch was quickly approaching, I realized things were running late. I was doing last-minute preparations when I remembered the rolls were still in the oven. As I grabbed an oven mitt and threw open

the oven door, a big blast of heat flew into my face. Closing my eyes to protect them, my mascara melted my eyes shut. This was really bad timing! I had to call Tony, who took over as I pried my eyes open. With mascara all over my face, I finished the lunch hour, catching periodic smirks from the wait staff. I never wore makeup in a kitchen again.

Warner Communications owned many businesses on the West Coast, but only Atari had an executive dining room. The chairs in the dining room were elite, cushioned and comfortable. Crisp linens were delivered weekly. Gorgeous flowers were delivered every Monday for use as centerpieces and bouquets. The waiters were professionally dressed in black and white suits. The food was served on fine china with crystal and silver, and a small supply of the finest wines was always available. Notable guests were frequently invited, including Mayor Dianne Feinstein of San Francisco, Joe Montana and Dwight Clark of the San Francisco 49ers, George Lucas and Steven Spielberg, Judy Collins and Peter Graves. I felt like I had arrived, preparing dinner for such well-known people.

The CEO of Warner Communications, Steven Ross, came to meet with the executives at Atari, which was quite an event. The side parking lot was cleared and blocked off for his arrival by helicopter. Tony was in contact with Mr. Ross's secretary, retrieving information about his favorite foods. We took several days planning precise menus. To my surprise, on the day of Mr. Ross's arrival, a bodyguard was appointed to watch me as I prepared the meals! To add insult to injury, the bodyguard was a chain smoker, which I found offensive in a public kitchen, and this was a three-day ordeal!

Occasionally Tony wanted to serve a buffet, and this was no small feast. Every buffet had a theme and the garde-manger created that theme. The first time I worked with Tony on a buffet I was overwhelmed at his talents. I had never seen food prepared so beautifully. Sensing the intensity in his work, I kept quiet, observed everything, and followed his exact instructions.

For the next buffet, I was in charge and chose a New England lobster feast for the California executives. A special order of clams,

oysters, and Maine lobster was flown in to the West Coast. I was using an old Maine lobster trap as a coffee table in my apartment, so that became the centerpiece, with shells from the Pacific shoreline as an accent. Fruit and vegetable carvings were used for garnishes and everything was served on silver trays. The creation of this New England lobster feast with a California twist was a representation of all I had learned and one of the highlights of my time at Atari.

Rich in so many ways and extremely rewarding, the four years in California were full of experiences of a lifetime. I grew way beyond my expectations personally and professionally. At the age of thirty-five, I had achieved what many chefs spend their whole lives trying to achieve. A New Englander at heart, though, I eventually longed for my family and the home I had left. With more expertise and experiences in cooking than I ever imagined possible, I packed my belongings and headed back to Massachusetts to begin another phase of my life.

Roquefort Tart

This was a popular appetizer served in the executive dining room at Atari.

Pastry
> 1¹/₄ cups flour
> 1 stick salted butter
> ¹/₄ teaspoon salt
> 3–4 tablespoons cold water

Filling
> 1 Roma tomato
> 1 shallot
> ¹/₃ cup Roquefort cheese

Custard
> 1 cup cream
> 4 eggs
> Dash nutmeg
> ¹/₄ teaspoon salt
> ¹/₄ teaspoon pepper

To make the pastry, put the flour, butter, and salt a food processor fitted with the blade and process until the mixture looks like fine crumbs. Slowly add the water until a ball of dough starts to form on the top of the blade. Press the dough into one large ball.

Preheat the oven to 400°F.

Roll out the dough to a 10-inch circle. Press the dough into a 9-inch fluted tart pan and trim the edges evenly. Refrigerate the

dough for 30 minutes. Bake the pie shell for 15 minutes. Remove from oven the and cool slightly. Lower the oven to 375°F.

For the filling, slice the tomato into thin rounds and line the bottom of the pie shell. Slice the shallot into thin rounds and place over the tomato. Sprinkle the Roquefort cheese over the vegetables.

For the custard, beat together the cream and eggs. Season with the nutmeg, salt, and pepper. Pour this mixture into the tart shell.

Bake for 30 minutes, or until the top is golden brown and a knife inserted into the center of the tart comes out clean. Serve warm or at room temperature as an appetizer or brunch.

Makes 8 servings as an appetizer, 4 servings as a brunch

Cook's Tip

Serve this tart as an appetizer or include as part of a company brunch.

Critic's Comments

Real men may not eat quiche, but they'll get in line for this tart! It tastes as good as it looks. The crust is better than any piecrust I've tasted!

—Marilyn Prell

Lemon Chicken

From Tony Dietz

2 whole boneless chicken breasts
$1/4$ cup cornstarch
3 tablespoons soy sauce
2 tablespoons dry white wine
3 egg yolks
$1/2$ teaspoon salt
$1/2$ teaspoon pepper

To dredge

1 cup cornstarch
$1/2$ cup flour

For the sauce

$1/2$ cup fresh lemon juice
$3/4$ cup water
$3/4$ cup sugar
$1 1/2$ tablespoons cornstarch
1 teaspoon salt

Cut the chicken into 1 inch julienne. Make a marinade by combining the ¼ cup cornstarch, soy sauce, white wine, egg yolks, salt, and pepper. Marinate the chicken, in the refrigerator, for several hours.

Mix the 1 cup of cornstarch and the flour. Dredge the chicken in this mixture and deep-fry, until golden brown.

Prepare the sauce by combining the lemon juice, water, sugar, cornstarch, and salt. Bring this mixture to a boil, then serve over the chicken.

Makes 4 servings

Crêpe Salsa

From Tony Dietz

8 crêpes
16 slices Monterey Jack cheese
Guacamole
Salsa sauce
Sour cream

Crêpes
$1/2$ cup flour
$3/4$ cup milk
2 eggs
2 tablespoons salted butter, melted
$1/2$ teaspoon salt

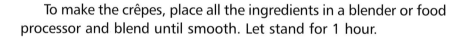

To make the crêpes, place all the ingredients in a blender or food processor and blend until smooth. Let stand for 1 hour.

Heat an 8-inch nonstick skillet pan over medium-high heat. Coat the pan with a little butter. Pour a scant $1/4$ cup of crêpe batter into the pan. Immediately tilt and rotate the pan until the batter forms a very thin layer on the bottom. Cook the crêpe until the top is set and the bottom is just beginning to turn golden. Shake the crêpe over the edge of the pan, and using your fingers, flip the crêpe and cook another minute. Remove from the pan and set on a plate or waxed paper.

Finish cooking the remaining batter, stacking the crêpes as they come out of the pan. Crêpes may be used right away or refrigerated for later use.

Guacamole

    4 ripe avocados
    1 can (4 ounces) diced green chilé
    1 medium-size tomato, diced
    2 tablespoons shallots, minced
    1 tablespoons garlic, minced
    1 tablespoon fresh lemon juice
    $1/2$ teaspoon salt
    $1/2$ teaspoon pepper

Cut the avocados in half lengthwise; twist to separate the halves. To remove the seed, use a large chef's knife. Stab the center of the seed with the center of the blade and twist. Scoop out the avocado pulp and put it in a bowl.

Using a wire whisk, mash the avocados, but keep them a bit chunky. Mix in the remaining ingredients. Cover the guacamole with plastic wrap to prevent discoloration. Refrigerate.

To assemble the crêpe salsa

Heat a 10-inch sauté pan over medium-high heat and coat with a little butter. Place a crêpe on the bottom of the pan, top with two slices of Monterey Jack cheese, and spread about $1/3$ cup of the guacamole over the cheese. When the crêpe starts to brown and the cheese begins to melt, fold the crêpe in half and again into quarters. Continue until the rest of the crêpes are done.

Serve garnished with the salsa sauce and sour cream.

Makes 8 servings

Cook's Tip

Keep crêpes warm in a 200°F oven until ready to serve; garnish just before serving.

Yakatori

Yakatori is the Japanese version of Chinese teriyaki.

$^1/_2$ cup dark Japanese soy sauce
$^1/_2$ cup dry sherry
2 tablespoons sugar
1 tablespoon minced gingerroot
1 garlic clove, minced
1 flank steak

Mix together the marinade ingredients. Add the steak and let sit overnight. Remove the steak from the marinade and pat dry; grill or broil about 8–9 minutes on each side for medium-rare, or until the desired doneness. Slice the steak against the grain on a long angle to achieve flat strips.

Makes 6 servings

Cook's Tips

I don't recommend marinating the steak for more than 24 hours, as the flavor will become too strong.

Use any tender cut of steak, such as steak tips or tenderloin.

Skinless, boneless chicken breast will work, too. Pat them dry from the marinade and brush with olive oil before you grill to prevent sticking to the grill.

Swordfish and tuna steaks are delicious in this marinade.

Use fresh ginger; it acts as a tenderizer and adds its own special flavor.

Critic's Comments

Flank steak is one of the leaner cuts of beef—thus, one of the more difficult to grill. This marinade, which features both soy sauce and garlic, perfectly tenderized the meat so that six of us on a lakeside night in Maine feasted on slices of hearty and flavorful beef. The marinade, a delicate blend of faintly discernible spices, imparted a deep mahogany finish to the exterior of the beef while making certain that the interior not only held in the entire flavor of real beef, but also maintained a texture reminiscent of a more richly marbled piece of meat.

All of us declared this recipe perfect. About the only suggestion my husband, the griller, and I could make was that whoever is grilling not be misled in figuring out when the meat is done by the lush finish imparted by the marinade.

—Barbara Simon

Lemon Thyme Marinade

2 cups fresh lemon juice
$1/2$ cup extra-virgin olive oil
2-inch piece peeled gingerroot, chopped
3 tablespoons thyme leaves
2 tablespoons minced garlic
2 teaspoons pepper
2 teaspoons salt
1–2 bay leaves, crumbled

Put all the ingredients in a bowl and blend.

Cook's Tips

Use this marinade for beef, veal, pork, lamb, chicken, turkey, swordfish, haddock, scallops, and shrimp.

Do not marinate more than 24 hours or the flavors will become too strong.

Makes $2^1/2$ cups

Critic's Comments

When I cook, there is always a clear and present danger that the meal will be ruined. I undercook chicken, overcook fish, burn the flavor out of steak—I've even made pasta float on the surface like bloated hot-air balloons. When Joan informed me that I would have to cook the marinated chicken myself, I instantly feared that I might cook the flavor out of the dish.

When I sat down to eat, I found that the meal was amazing. Most marinades have a fading tang, but this lemon-thyme mix lasted the entire meal, and each bite was evenly flavored. It made even my horrible cooking skills seem on par with the great chefs of the world. The perfect mix of flavor, I could see this marinade as a delicious complement to fish, too.

—Brian Deveney

Tomato Sauce

From Tony Dietz

This recipe has all the elements of a great tomato sauce. Make in quantity and freeze or can for later use.

1/2 pound bacon, diced
8 large onions, finely diced
1 large bunch celery, finely diced
1/4 cup fresh minced garlic
2 tablespoons rosemary
2 tablespoons thyme
1 tablespoon oregano
1 teaspoon cayenne
2 tablespoons sugar
1 tablespoon basil
1 cup flour
1 #10 can diced tomatoes
1 #10 can tomato purée
1 1/2 gallons beef stock
1 quart burgundy wine
1 large ham hock or 2 small hocks
1/4 cup Worcestershire sauce
2 bay leaves

In a 16-quart stockpot, sauté the bacon until it is crisp and the fat has rendered. Add the onions, celery, and garlic; cook over medium-high heat for 30–45 minutes, or until the vegetables caramelize. Add the spices and the sugars and stir to blend.

Add the flour to make a roux. Bind with the tomatoes, tomato purée, beef stock, and wine.

Add the ham hock, the Worcestershire sauce, and the bay leaves and simmer, uncovered, for 2 hours.

Strain and adjust the seasoning.

Makes 3$^1/_2$ gallons

Cook's Tips

This recipe makes about 3 gallons. It is a bit time consuming, but well worth the effort.

Instead of straining the sauce, purée in the food processor and keep in all the good vegetables. They will add substance to the sauce.

I use a small daisy ham instead of the ham hocks. A ham bone will add the same smoky flavor.

Spaetzle

Being that Tony Dietz was German, he taught me how to make great spaetzle, a German noodle.

3 cups flour
6 eggs
$1/2$ cup milk
Pinch of salt
$1/2$ stick butter

Using a wire whip, blend the flour, eggs, milk, and salt. Allow the mixture to rest for 1 hour.

Set a spaetzle maker over a pot of boiling salted water and drop the batter into the hopper. Slowly slide the hopper back and forth, allowing the batter to drip into the water. Do not slide the hopper beyond the spaetzle maker, as you will have a mess on the stove.

Boil the spaetzle, stirring occasionally, for 3 to 4 minutes, or until they float to the top and turn whitish in color; drain and chill.

Melt the butter in a sauté pan and add the spaetzle. Sprinkle with salt and pepper and a little nutmeg. Sauté until the noodles are golden brown; serve plain or with gravy.

Makes 6 servings

Cook's Tips

Be sure to chill the spaetzle before sautéing, as they will mash.

Spaetzle can be served plain with butter, salt, and pepper, but I think the extra sautéing is worth the effort.

Season the spaetzle batter with your favorite herbs and spices.

Ginger-Pineapple Chutney

1 pineapple cut into chunks
1 cup brown sugar, packed
1 cup granulated sugar
1 cup golden raisins
1 small onion, finely diced
2$\frac{1}{2}$ ounces peeled gingerroot,
    finely diced

3 large garlic cloves,
    finely diced
$\frac{3}{4}$ cup white wine vinegar
2 teaspoons mustard seed
1–2 teaspoons crushed red
    pepper flakes
1$\frac{1}{2}$ teaspoons salt

Put all the ingredients in a large pot and simmer for 25 to 30 minutes, or until the sauce thickens. Chill, then serve with grilled meats, poultry, or seafood.

Makes about 1 quart

Cook's Tips

You can purchase fresh pineapple, peeled and cored, in the produce department of many grocery stores.

Substitute fresh Italian prune plums for the pineapple.

Critic's Comments

No one has ever been able to sell me on chutney. When Joan asked me to try this side dish alone and on chicken, I responded with a hesitant yes. I didn't want to write a negative report. It turned out that I didn't have to.

The chutney has a great sweet flavor with a spicy kick. It's that spicy kick that enticed me. It's a great addition to any meal or crackers. Now I find myself entering a new stage in life, one where there will be chutney, or at least Joan's chutney, on the table.

—Brian Deveney

Spinach Salad with Chutney Dressing

This salad is easy and popular with everyone. The dressing lends itself to a variety of greens and garnishes.

1 pound baby spinach leaves
2 hard-cooked eggs
4 slices cooked bacon

Dressing
$1/2$ cup red wine vinegar
$1/3$ cup Major Grey chutney
2 whole cloves of garlic
$1/4$ cup whole-grain mustard
1 cup extra-virgin olive oil
1 teaspoon sugar

Wash and thoroughly dry the spinach leaves. Chop the eggs and dice the bacon. Place on top of the spinach.

To make the dressing, put the vinegar, chutney, mustard, garlic, and sugar in a food processor and process until smooth. Slowly pour in the olive oil until the dressing emulsifies.

Pour the dressing over the spinach, toss, and serve. Garnish with more diced egg and bacon, if desired.

Makes 8 servings as a side dish, 4 servings as a main dish

Cook's Tips

Although any chutney can be used, I like Major Grey's Mango Chutney.

Grey Poupon can be substituted for the whole-grain mustard.

Substitute canned mandarin oranges and sliced almonds for the egg and bacon.

Use this dressing for chicken salad or potato salad. Be creative.

Eliminate the sugar and add up to $1/2$ cup of chutney for a fruitier flavor.

Critic's Comments

This is a novel take on a traditional salad favorite. Chock-full of crispy bacon and chopped hard-cooked egg, the salad gets its character from the tangy mango-chutney dressing, an almost perfect blend of sweet and tart. The dressing is a summer ragweed yellow and owes its sweet to the chutney and its tart to whole-grain mustard. The salad is pleasing at the end of a summer day as a meal in itself. In cooler weather, it would make a great accompaniment to soup.

—Barbara Simon

Vinaigrette

From Tony Dietz

Salads are integral to meals in California, and the dressings are just as important. The following salad dressings are among my favorites.

1 cup red wine vinegar
2 tablespoons garlic-flavored oil
1 tablespoon salt
1 teaspoon pepper
Extra-virgin olive oil

Using a clean wine bottle, funnel in the red vinegar, garlic oil, salt, and pepper. Shake thoroughly to dissolve the salt. Add enough olive oil to fill the bottle, about 3 cups. Replace the cork and store until ready to use on any garden salad.

Makes 1 quart

Cook's Tips

This dressing will last several months in the refrigerator.

Use 750 ml empty bottles of wine to make flavored oils, vinegars, and salad dressings.

To make your own garlic-flavored oil, place 5 or 6 sliced cloves of fresh garlic in an empty wine bottle. Fill the bottle with olive oil, cork, and let the garlic flavor infuse the oil for 24 hours before using. Store in the refrigerator.

Always use a good-quality olive oil for salad dressings.

Flavor oils with hot peppers, herbs, and your favorite spices.

Flavor vinegars by adding strawberries, raspberries, blueberries, or other fruits.

Creamy Italian Dressing

From Tony Dietz

2 cups mayonnaise
1 recipe of Vinaigrette (see page 144)
1 cup heavy cream

Put the mayonnaise in the work bowl of a heavy-duty mixer. Using the wire whip attachment, begin beating the mayonnaise on high. Very slowly, pour the Vinaigrette into the mayonnaise to form an emulsion.

Whisk in the heavy cream and chill. Serve on any garden salad.

Makes 1 1/2 quarts

Cook's Tip

This dressing will last one month in the refrigerator.

Store the salad dressing in an empty bottle of wine.

Bleu Cheese Salad Dressing

From Tony Dietz

8 ounces cream cheese
8–10 ounces bleu cheese, crumbled
1 quart mayonnaise
2 cups sour cream
1 small onion, finely diced
1 cup red wine vinegar
2 tablespoons Worcestershire sauce
Couple of drops Tabasco

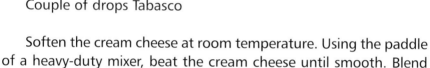

Soften the cream cheese at room temperature. Using the paddle of a heavy-duty mixer, beat the cream cheese until smooth. Blend in the remaining ingredients.

Makes 2 quarts

Cook's Tips

This dressing will last for one month in the refrigerator.

Store the salad dressing in a covered, plastic container.

Thin the dressing with water if it becomes too thick.

You can use low-fat varieties of cream cheese, sour cream, and mayonnaise, but I do not recommend fat-free; the taste and texture are just not the same.

Add enough bleu cheese to your taste.

Use a good-quality bleu cheese such as Maytag or Point Reyes.

Herbed Vinaigrette

Although this dressing is a bit more involved, the result is worth it.

1 red onion
4 cloves fresh garlic
$1/2$ bunch fresh parsley, leaves only
1 tablespoon horseradish
1 tablespoon whole-grain mustard
1 tablespoon dried tarragon
$1^1/_2$ teaspoons salt
$1^1/_2$ teaspoons black pepper
$1^1/_2$ teaspoons white pepper
1 cup red wine vinegar
$2^1/_2$ cups peanut oil
1 cup olive oil

Put the red onion, garlic, parsley, horseradish, mustard, tarragon, and the salt and peppers in the bowl of a food processor. Pulse until finely chopped. Transfer to a bowl and add the vinegar. Let this mixture steep for 1 to 2 hours, then strain.

Add the peanut oil and the olive oil to the vinegar and chill.

Makes 5 cups

Cook's Tips

This dressing will last for several months in the refrigerator.

Store the dressing in an empty bottle of wine.

Use the chopped herbed mixture to flavor meat dishes such as beef and lamb.

For special occasions, I spread the herbed mixture over a leg of lamb, then roast it in the oven.

Add a bottle of Pinot Noir to the herb mixture and simmer until the wine is reduced by half. Pour this over a leg of lamb, cover, and braise in a 300°F oven for 3 to 4 hours, or until the meat is tender and falling off the bone.

San Francisco Cheesecake

1½ cups graham cracker crumbs
4 tablespoons butter, melted
½ teaspoon cinnamon
1½ pounds cream cheese, at room temperature
1 cup plus 3 tablespoons sugar
4 eggs
2 yolks
Juice and rind of 1 lemon
1½ cups sour cream
1½ teaspoons vanilla

Preheat the oven to 300°F.

Mix together the graham cracker crumbs, butter, and cinnamon. Transfer to a 9-inch spring-form pan. Using the back of a spoon, pat the crumbs down on the bottom and halfway up the sides of the pan. Set aside.

Using a heavy-duty mixer fitted with a paddle, beat the cream cheese until soft and smooth, 2 minutes. Add 1 cup of the sugar and beat 2 minutes more. One at a time, beat in the eggs and egg yolks.

Blend in the lemon juice and rind. Pour this mixture into the spring-form pan and bake for 1 hour, or until the center of the cake has set. Remove from oven and let cool for 10 minutes.

Heat the oven to 350°F. Blend together the sour cream, the remaining 3 tablespoons of the sugar, and the vanilla. With a rubber scraper, gently spread the sour cream mixture over the cheesecake. Return the cheesecake to the oven and cook for another 10 minutes. Cool to room temperature, then refrigerate. Serve cold.

Makes 8 servings

Cook's Tips

To make graham cracker crumbs, process the crackers in a food processor.

Graham crackers come in chocolate flavor and can be substituted for regular graham crackers.

Try vanilla wafer crumbs for the crust to a cheesecake.

Add $1/4$ cup nuts (walnuts, almonds, or pecans) to the food processor when making the cracker crumbs for heightened flavor.

Substitute your favorite liqueur, such as Grand Marnier, Bailey's Irish Cream, Kahlua, or Chambord, for the lemon juice.

Use melted dark, milk, or white chocolate instead of the lemon juice.

Always bake cheesecake at a low temperature for just the right amount of time to prevent cracking on top. Regardless of what a recipe says, I always bake my cheesecakes at 300°F for no more than 1 hour.

Critic's Comments

There is only one word to describe this cheesecake: *decadent*. The sweet and creamy filling is far superior to any you could hope to find in gourmet restaurants. This sweetness is complemented perfectly by the slightly tart hint of lemon. The top layer, along with this subtle lemon flavor, causes the taster to be reminded of a lemon meringue pie. All the best qualities of a cheesecake and lemon meringue intermingle to form this delectable treat. Consider garnishing with fresh raspberries to flatter these flavors even further.

—Jenifer Pellerin

Christmas Eve White Chocolate Mousse Parfait

As a pastry cook, I prepared this white chocolate mousse and presented it in a variety of ways: frozen and garnished with fruit, nuts, and sauces; in layers between cakes; piped into pâte à choux; and spread into puff pastry squares. I traditionally serve this dessert on Christmas Eve. I spoon the mousse into parfait glasses in layers with Maine's Bartlett red raspberry wine and garnish it with a raspberry shortcake cookie on page 232. What a way to end your meal or any celebration!

12 ounces white chocolate, chopped
$1/4$ cup heavy cream
1 stick salted butter
6 egg yolks
$2^1/2$ cups heavy cream, whipped
Sweet raspberry wine

Heat the chocolate, $1/4$ cup heavy cream, butter, and yolks slowly over low to medium heat in a double boiler, until the chocolate melts. Beat lightly to emulsify, then let cool slightly.

Fold the $2^1/2$ cups of whipped cream into the chocolate mixture and refrigerate overnight until firm.

In parfait glasses, layer the mousse with a sweet after-dinner wine. Garnish with a raspberry shortcake cookie.

Makes 8 servings

Critics' Comments

A seemingly decadent holiday treat that is just as good in the middle of the summer as it is on Christmas Eve, this combination of white chocolate mousse and layers of a raspberry apéritif creates a bold red- and-white image that tastes as good as it looks. The lightness of the mousse combined with the fruitiness of the wine makes a perfect dessert for an outstanding dinner.

—Peg and Marty Stout

Oatmeal Cookies

I made these oatmeal cookies by the dozens every day for years for the executive dining room at Atari.

2 sticks salted butter
$^3/_4$ cup brown sugar, packed
$^1/_2$ cup granulated sugar
1 egg
1 teaspoon vanilla
$^3/_4$ cup light cream
3 cups oats
$1^1/_2$ cups flour
$^1/_2$ cup shredded coconut
1 teaspoon baking soda
1 teaspoon cinnamon
$^1/_2$ teaspoon salt
$^1/_4$ teaspoon nutmeg

Preheat the oven to 375°F.

Cream the butter and sugars. Beat in the egg and vanilla. Blend in the light cream.

Blend in the remaining ingredients. Shape the cookies onto an ungreased sheet pan using a #30 ice-cream scoop; bake for 12 to 15 minutes, or until the center of the cookies are golden brown. Cool on a rack.

Makes 18 cookies

Critic's Comments

These are "cookie monster" cookies! The rich blended flavors melted on my taste buds and left a lingering aftertaste to savor. The soft texture didn't crumble on the first or last bite, either. Warm or cool, these cookies *taste* homemade.

—Marilyn Prell

CHAPTER FIVE

Teaching at Timberlane

Teaching at Timberlane

Upon returning to the East Coast, I did some freelancing at various restaurants, continuing to refine my talents. Eventually, the long days, nights, weekends, and holidays in the kitchen took their toll, as I missed spending time with family and friends. Browsing through the Boston Sunday *Globe* one day, I noticed an opening for a cooking teacher at a high school in southern New Hampshire. During the interview, it was made clear to me that the program was suffering, and that if it wasn't revised it would be canceled. I accepted the position and felt prepared for my next challenge.

The classroom was an old-fashioned home economics room with five kitchen stations and no professional equipment. With the vision of what I had done at Atari, I prepared a plan to change the classroom into a restaurant and offer lunch and catering services to the faculty and administration. Slowly the curriculum changed to offer full-year courses in basic foods and nutrition, expanding with courses on more advanced cooking techniques. To attract students, I renamed the courses Culinary Classics and Gourmet Foods. Baking and Pastries was added later.

Working with the facility I had, my students began serving the faculty lunch every Thursday, with a reservation list of twenty-five staff members. We turned the six tables in the classroom into a dining room, covering them with tablecloths and decorating with dried flower centerpieces. Each of the five kitchen stations had a purpose: The sauté station cooked the food; the line station plated the food; the pastry station prepared and plated the desserts; there was a dishwasher station and a waiter station. The students responded well to these changes and seemed to really enjoy serving lunch to their teachers.

With higher enrollments, the administration gave me a larger budget. Shopping at a restaurant supply store, I purchased dinner plates, glasses, and silverware; as the years went on more professional equipment was added to the classroom. The program gained in popularity with students and faculty; today the reservation list

stands at seventy-five and more students than can be accommodated sign up for the course each year.

Gourmet Foods is a full-year program studying American regional foods during the fall semester and international foods in spring. Culinary Classics is a prerequisite. Every Thursday the faculty and staff are served a gourmet meal consisting of an entrée, a couple of side dishes, fresh rolls, and dessert.

Local chefs have been very responsive in coming to visit Gourmet Foods, and many have acted as guest chef preparing meals with the students. Guest chef Maria, from L'Esprit, in Dover, New Hampshire, prepared the classic beef Wellington with all the fine details, side dishes, and vanilla crème brûlée for dessert. With amazement, the students flambéed the top of the brûlée with a kitchen torch. Having lunch at L'Espirit, the students marveled over the presentation of their meals, especially dessert. As a result, Gourmet Foods now presents showcase desserts to the faculty.

Occasionally, school functions require catering services, for which I rely on my experiences at Atari. Timberlane High School has hosted the New Hampshire All-State Jazz Festival, during which the Gourmet Foods students operate a hospitality room for the directors. A highlighted event, students prepare all meals—including soups, salads, breads, snacks, and desserts—for three days. The buffet and dining room tables are adorned with fresh flower arrangements and the room inspires great energy. The response and compliments from the directors are always overwhelming.

One year I had the ultimate Gourmet Foods class. Even though the students had diverse personalities, everyone bonded and worked as a team. As problems arose, we solved them together. Around the holidays, the students prepared a gourmet meal for themselves, arranging tables, laying out tablecloths, and using our best dishes as everyone ate together. There was the annual field trip to the Mango Grill and a special field trip was planned for Perkins Cove in Ogunquit, Maine. We walked the Marginal Way, climbed the rocks, browsed through the shops, took lots of pictures, and had lunch at the Hurricane Restaurant.

At the end of the school year, after graduation, the entire class came back to pay me a special tribute. I was touched and cried. I love these kids: Dawn Bowley, Eric Bradley, Shawn Bragg, Crystal Briere, Lindsay Brown, Craig Daigle, Erin Devine, Christopher Doherty, Jake Guide, Jenny Jacobson, Patrick Kenney, Laura Rollins, Leslie Roy, Gina Sarno, Mike Swarbrick, and Barry Weinhold.

One student I have a particular fondness for is Anthony Jackson. A.J. had a natural talent for cooking. He spent three years with me before continuing his education at the Culinary Institute of America, New York. After graduating from the institute, A.J. wanted to return something to his high school, and he spent every Friday teaching my students his newly learned trade with demonstrations and tastings. He was an extremely popular young man with a wonderful sense of humor, and the students always looked forward to his weekly visits.

Shawn Bragg was definitely one of my favorites. He approached me in his sophomore year to inform me that he didn't need to take Culinary Classics, that his skills were beyond that course. We fought over this for several weeks and, well, I lost! Shawn joined Gourmet Foods and was there for the next three years. His cooking skills were good. His personality kept everyone entertained, especially me. Above that, Shawn could fix anything. There was a Coke machine in my room and frequently something was not working, and sure enough, Shawn could fix it. Today Shawn is married to his high school sweetheart, Christine. They have two lovely little girls, and ironically Shawn works for the Coca Cola Company repairing vending machines.

I have learned a great deal from my colleagues and especially from my students. They have shared their family stories, heritages, and recipes. My students have been some of my best teachers and have made my professional life extremely rewarding.

Chili Dip

From Jeff Watjen, a former student

1 medium onion, chopped
1 clove garlic, minced
Olive oil
1 pound ground beef
2–4 teaspoons chili powder
1 teaspoon salt
1/2 teaspoon oregano
1 can (16 ounces) whole tomatoes, undrained
1 can (15 ounces) red kidney beans, drained
1 can (8 ounces) tomato sauce
1 tablespoon red wine vinegar
1 pound cream cheese, softened
1 pound shredded Mexican cheese
Tortilla chips

To make the chili, sauté the onion and garlic in a little olive oil in a large saucepan. Add ground beef and sauté until the meat is no longer pink. Add the chili powder, salt, oregano, whole tomatoes, kidney beans, tomato sauce, and vinegar. Let simmer for 30 minutes.

Preheat the oven to 350°F.

Spread the cream cheese on the bottom of an 8x13 inch ovenproof dish.

Spread the chili on top of the cream cheese. Sprinkle the shredded Mexican cheese on top of the chili. Bake for 15 to 20 minutes, or until the cheese is hot and bubbling. Serve with the tortilla chips.

Makes 8–10 servings

Sausage Soup

From Rita Piazza, a colleague

1 onion, chopped
1 clove garlic, minced
Olive oil
1 can (28 ounces) Hunts tomato sauce
$1^1/_2$ cups water
Salt and pepper
1 pound sweet sausage
$^1/_4$ cup orzo

Sauté the onion and garlic in a little olive oil. Add the tomato sauce and water. Add salt and pepper to taste.

Cut the sausage into small pieces. Add to the soup and simmer until the sausage is cooked, about 15 to 20 minutes. Add the orzo, cover, and simmer for 10 minutes. Let the soup stand for 15 minutes, covered, with the heat off.

Makes 4 servings

Cook's Tips

Substitute rice for the orzo.

Add chopped spinach to the soup for added flavor and color.

Cut sausage while frozen into thin rounds.

Purchase lean, quality sausage from an Italian deli.

Cream of Artichoke Soup

From Jeannine Alexander, a former student

6 tablespoons salted butter or olive oil
6 tablespoons finely chopped onion
6 tablespoons flour
6 cups chicken broth
4 cans (15 ounces) artichoke hearts, drained
4 tablespoons fresh lemon juice
1 teaspoon salt
1/4 teaspoon pepper
1/4 teaspoon dried thyme leaves
2 cups light cream

Melt the butter in a large saucepan. Sauté the onion until tender, about 5 minutes. Stir in the flour to make a roux and cook, stirring constantly, for 5 to 8 minutes, or until the roux turns a golden brown.

Whisk in the chicken broth and bring to a simmer. Quarter the artichoke hearts and add them to the broth, along with the lemon juice, salt, pepper, and thyme. Simmer 20 to 30 minutes, then stir in the cream.

Serve hot or cold.

Makes 8 servings

Cook's Tips

Olive oil is healthier for you, but butter tastes good. You choose!

I add a little more onion to enhance the flavor.

Be sure to simmer the soup for 20 to 30 minutes to cook out the pasty taste of the flour.

Use between 2 and 4 tablespoons of fresh lemon juice or to taste.

I coarsely chop the artichokes rather than quarter them; it's a personal preference.

Add up to 1 teaspoon of thyme for a more pronounced flavor.

If the soup is to be served cold or is too thick, thin with more chicken stock.

Critic's Comments

If you're a fan of artichokes and cream soups, this is the perfect soup for you. It's a thick mixture, replete with artichokes. I detected a mild flavoring of lemon that gave the soup a bit more zest than some of the less ambitious cream soups. The soup can be served cold, as a meal in the summer, or warm. When it is served cold, the attractive cool green of the artichokes enhances the eye appeal of the soup; when the soup is served warm, however, the soup is a good bit thinner, which encouraged this taster to eat way too much.

Because this is such a thick soup, I would probably most enjoy it as a first course in a small serving before an elegant entrée, as the cream and artichokes speak of fine dining.

—Barbara Simon

Eggplant Frittata

From Tony Hanscome, a colleague

2 large eggplants, peeled and cubed
3 cups water
1–2 cups Italian seasoned bread crumbs
8 or 9 eggs
1/2 cup olive oil
1/2 cup grated Parmesan cheese
1/2 cup fresh parsley, chopped
1 tablespoon basil
1 tablespoon oregano
2 teaspoons garlic powder
2 teaspoons onion powder
1 teaspoon salt
1/2 teaspoon marjoram
1/2 teaspoon pepper
1/8 teaspoon cayenne

Put the eggplant in a large pot with the water and boil until soft, about 10 minutes, then allow to cool.

Preheat the oven to 350°F.

Add enough bread crumbs to soak up the water. Add the remaining ingredients and blend in.

Generously brush a sheet pan with olive oil. Spread the eggplant mixture to brownie thickness all over the pan. Bake until the top is golden, 40 to 50 minutes.

Slide the eggplant out of the pan onto a cutting board. With a pizza cutter, cut into squares.

Makes 12 servings

Cook's Tip

Serve as an appetizer, side dish or for a company brunch.

Add seasonings to taste; the more the better.

Cajun Baked Haddock

Jason Craib, a former student

One year my student Jason Craib asked me if he could do some extra-credit work by preparing a dish for the class. He brought in some haddock (fish is not real popular with teenagers), made a marinade, and baked the fish. His classmates changed their opinion of fish after tasting this dish. I have even served this to the faculty and received great reviews. Flavorful and a bit spicy, this is easy to make.

1/2 stick salted butter
2 tablespoons barbecue sauce
2 tablespoons fresh lemon juice
1/2 teaspoon basil
1/2 teaspoon paprika
1/2 teaspoon rosemary
1/4 teaspoon crushed red pepper
1 bay leaf
1 clove garlic, minced
1 1/2 pounds haddock

Preheat the oven to 450°F.

Melt the butter. Add the barbecue sauce, lemon juice, and the herbs and spices. Simmer for 5 minutes, then remove the bay leaf. Cool slightly.

Pour the sauce over the fish in a casserole dish and bake for about 15 minutes, or until the fish flakes.

Makes 4 servings

Cook's Tips

A great way to cook fish is at a high temperature (450°F) for a short period of (15 minutes). The fish cooks fast and stays moist, and the sugars in the barbecue sauce caramelize.

Use any whitefish: cod, halibut, sole, swordfish, scallops, or shrimp.

The marinade is excellent over chicken or pork chops, baked in a 350°F oven for 40 to 45 minutes.

Critics' Comments

Know your audience when you prepare this New Orleans version of a traditional Maine entrée! The delicate blend of barbecue sauce and spices on large fresh chunks of haddock produces a succulent, spicy, delicious dish for those who enjoy "a little spice" in their lives! The level of spiciness can be changed, depending on the taste buds of your guests.

—Peg and Marty Stout

Maple-Soy Salmon

From Cheryl McDonough, a colleague

1 pound salmon fillet, skinned and boned
1 tablespoon fresh lemon juice
1 tablespoon maple syrup
1 tablespoon soy sauce
Dash of nutmeg

Place the salmon in an ovenproof casserole. Mix together the lemon juice, maple syrup, and soy sauce and pour over the fish. Sprinkle lightly with the nutmeg. Let marinate for about 1 hour.

Preheat the oven to 400°F.

Bake the salmon for 15 to 20 minutes, or until the fish flakes.

Makes 4 servings

Cook's Tips

The marinade ingredients should glaze, not soak, the salmon.

Nutmeg is a very powerful spice, so sprinkle lightly.

Use quality soy sauce and maple syrup; it really makes a difference.

Fettuccini with Chicken and Pesto

From Derek Reardon, a former student

1 pound boneless chicken breasts
Salt and pepper
1 tablespoon extra virgin olive oil
1 jar (7 ounces) roasted red peppers
1¼ cups heavy cream
⅓ cup prepared pesto
12 ounces fettuccini
Grated Parmesan cheese

Cut the chicken into thin strips and season with the salt and pepper.

In a large skillet, heat the olive oil and thoroughly cook the chicken, turning frequently, about 10 minutes.

Drain the roasted peppers and chop. Add to the chicken and cook 1 minute. Add the cream and simmer until thickened, 3 to 5 minutes. Remove from heat and stir in the pesto. Taste and adjust the salt.

Cook the fettuccini until al dente and toss with the chicken mixture. Sprinkle with the Parmesan cheese.

Makes 4 servings

Cook's Tips

Substitute parboiled broccoli flowerets, for the roasted red peppers.
Roast your own peppers by rubbing them with olive oil, then

put on a sheet pan in a 450°F oven for 20 to 30 minutes, or until the skins are charred and blistering. Allow to cool; discard the seeds and skin. Their flavor is unsurpassed!

You can reduce the fat in this recipe by omitting the heavy cream.

Chicken-Wrapped Stuffed Poblano Peppers

Justin Shatler is truly gifted. He is a natural-born cook teaching himself through hands-on experience. Justin was my student for three years at Timberlane High School. After graduation, he continued his culinary career with an old-fashioned apprenticeship.

Throughout high school, Justin worked at a pizza parlor learning the basics, especially knife skills. He chopped, sliced, and diced by hand many vegetables for salads, sandwiches, and pizzas. He learned how to make pizza dough—the kneading, rising, and shaping. He also learned the importance of speed in a professional kitchen.

His progression led him to Joseph's Trattoria in Haverhill, Massachusetts, where his knowledge expanded. When a Caribbean restaurant opened in North Andover, Massachusetts, Justin changed jobs and there he was encouraged to develop his creativity. The owners provided him with excellent guidance and tremendous opportunity.

Every year I take my advanced students to dinner at the Mango Grill in North Andover. We get a tour of the open kitchen with its wood-burning oven. We experience Justin's fine cooking, tasting unfamiliar flavors. One year Justin came to my classroom as a guest chef and directed my students in preparing a flavorful, spicy chicken-wrapped poblano pepper. He did so without a recipe. Everything came out of his head and into his hands. There were no measurements; he added a little of this and a little of that, tasting frequently and readjusting to please his palate.

Creativity is what I try to teach my students. A recipe is only a guideline. Food will taste different from producer to producer, from cook to cook. One chicken tastes different from another depending on what it was fed. One fruit tastes different from another depending on its growing conditions. Wines taste different from

winery to winery depending when the grapes were picked, the weather, and where they are grown. You can't simply follow a recipe; you must taste.

The proportions in this recipe are the ones that please me.

$1/2$ pound andouille sausage
2 ears corn
1 bunch scallions, diced
$1/2$ pound Monterey Jack cheese, grated
4 poblano peppers
4 half chicken breasts
Fresh bread crumbs

Preheat the oven to 400°F.

Place the sausage in a food processor fitted with the blade and pulse until it is coarsely chopped. Transfer to a large bowl.

Husk the corn and cut off the kernels. Place the corn kernels on a sheet pan and roast for about 10 minutes, or until the corn starts to turn a golden brown. Add to the sausage, along with the scallions and cheese. Mix and set aside.

Preheat an oven to 450°F. Place the peppers on a sheet pan and drizzle with a little olive oil. Roast until the skins are charred, 20 to 30 minutes. Remove from the oven and allow to cool. Very carefully cut a slit down the side of each pepper and remove the seeds. Keep the peppers intact, working gracefully. Take a handful of the filling and carefully stuff the peppers.

Lower the oven to 400°F.

Pound the chicken breasts evenly to $1/4$ inch and wrap one breast around each pepper.

Spray a sheet pan lightly with oil. Place the chicken seam-side down and roast for 15 minutes. Remove the chicken from the oven and sprinkle with the bread crumbs. Return the chicken to the oven for another 5 to 10 minutes, until the crumbs are golden and the chicken is cooked.

Serve the chicken drizzled with Chipotle Vinaigrette (see page 176).

Makes 4 servings

Cook's Tips

I always use Bell and Evans chickens. They are free-range and taste the way a chicken ought to taste.

I buy andouille sausage from North Country Smokehouse in Claremont, New Hampshire.

Kielbasa or linguica can be substituted for the andouille sausage.

Fresh is better, but frozen corn can be used.

Do roast the corn, as it caramelizes its natural sugars, thus adding depth to the flavor of the stuffing.

Scallions have a milder flavor than onions and add color to the stuffing.

Monterey Jack is a mild cheese; other Cheddars could be substituted.

Sweet green peppers will work, but poblanos have a more distinctive flavor.

Use fresh, not dried, Italian bread crumbs, which will make a nicer crust and stick to the chicken better.

Critics' Comments

This unique chicken dish is worth the extra effort it takes to prepare. Sliced wedges of chicken showing swirls of stuffed peppers make a classy presentation full of robust flavors.

—Peg and Marty Stout

Chipotle Vinaigrette

Justin told me to blend these ingredients in any proportions until I was satisfied. I watched him make the vinaigrette by randomly pouring ingredients into a blender and tasting repeatedly until it was good to him. The following tastes good to me.

1 can (7 ounces) chipotle peppers with sauce
$1/2$ cup olive oil
3 tablespoons Rose's lime juice
1 tablespoon honey
$1/2$ teaspoon chili powder
Salt and pepper

Put all the ingredients in a blender and process until smooth. Adjust flavors to your taste.

Makes 1 cup

Cook's Tips

Add cayenne for more heat.

This vinaigrette will keep for one month in the refrigerator.

Critics' Comments

This versatile vinaigrette can serve as a variation for many familiar sauces: a cocktail sauce for shrimp, barbecue sauce for chicken or beef, a sauce to serve over an entrée, to name just a few. In spite of the chipotle peppers and chili powder combination, it's only mildly spicy, tempered by the honey and lime juice, but it has a pungent aroma with a slight bite.

—Peg and Marty Stout

Portuguese Pot Roast

From Roxanne O'Connor, a colleague

3–4 pound chuck roast
Beef stock or water
1 onion, sliced
Juice from 1 jar (22 ounce) sweet mixed pickles
1 pound carrots, peeled and cut into chunks
1 package brown gravy mix
1 can (28 ounce) whole tomatoes
1 package (16 ounces) frozen green beans
1 pound potatoes, peeled and cut into chunks
Pinch of sugar

Sear the meat on both sides in a hot skillet until browned and crispy. Add enough beef stock or to just barely cover the meat. Add the onion and pickle juice. Lower the heat and simmer, covered, until the meat is tender, 2 to 2$^1/_2$ hours.

Add the carrots to the meat, along with the gravy mix, tomatoes, and green beans. Simmer to thicken the gravy, about 10 minutes.

Add the potatoes and simmer for 30 to 45 minutes, or until the potatoes are soft. Add a pinch of sugar to adjust the acidity.

Makes 8 servings

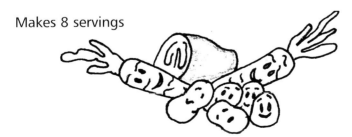

Italian Meat Roll

From Christopher Cirella, a former student

1 pound hamburger
1 cup bread crumbs
1 cup Parmesan cheese, grated
1 egg
2 tablespoons water
1/4 cup chopped parsley
1 onion, diced
1 hard-cooked egg, chopped
1 quart seasoned tomato sauce

Mix together the hamburger, bread crumbs, cheese, egg and water. Roll out the hamburger into an 8x10 inch rectangle.

Sprinkle the meat with the parsley, onion and hard-cooked egg. Roll up the meat jellyroll-style and broil on a broiler pan until crispy, carefully turning and rolling over the meat.

Transfer the meat roll to a saucepan and add the well-seasoned tomato sauce. Simmer for 1 hour.

Slice the meat roll and serve with your favorite pasta.

Makes 4 servings

Cook's Tip

Lay slices of Genoa salami and Provolone cheese on the meat before rolling.

Pork and Rice Pilaf

From Jodie Needham, a former student

3 slices bacon, diced
1 pound pork loin, diced
1 large onion, diced
1 cup uncooked rice
3 cups water
1 teaspoon salt
$1/2$ teaspoon black pepper
1 red bell pepper

Sauté the bacon until crispy. Remove the bacon bits and set aside. Add the pork and onion to the bacon drippings and sauté until brown.

Wash the rice under cold running water until the water runs clear. Add to the pork mixture and sauté until opaque, 2 to 3 minutes. Add the water, salt, and black pepper. Cover and simmer for 10 minutes.

Remove the seeds from the red pepper and finely dice. Add to the rice, along with the reserved bacon bits. Simmer, covered, for an additional 10 minutes, or until the rice is soft and the water has been absorbed.

Makes 4 servings

Kielbasa in the Crock-pot®

From Gail Wozniak, a colleague

The faculty at Timberlane high school frequently organized potluck lunches. Gail always brought this dish, and it was the first to go.

    2 pounds kielbasa
    2 jars (12–18 ounces) apple jelly
    1 tablespoon whole cloves
    French's yellow mustard

Place the jelly in a Crock-pot® and turn on low. Stir in the cloves.

Cut the kielbasa into $1/4$ inch slices and add to the jelly mixture. Squirt the mustard in a $1/4$ inch-wide circle around the inside perimeter of the pot and stir it in. The mustard is just to cut the sweetness of the jelly; add as little or as much as you like.

Cook on low for about 2 hours, stirring every half hour. Serve as soon as it is hot.

Makes 6–8 servings

Cook's Tip

This is a great dish to serve as an hors d' oeuvre at a cocktail party.

Barbecue Sauce for Spare Ribs

From Karen LaBelle, a former student

$1/2$ cup onion, chopped
Olive oil
1 cup chili sauce
$3/4$ cup crushed pineapple in syrup
$1/3$ cup fresh lemon juice
$1/4$ cup brown sugar, packed
3 tablespoons Worcestershire sauce
$1/2$ teaspoon powdered ginger
$1/8$ teaspoon salt
3 pounds spare ribs
Garlic powder

Preheat the oven to 350°F.

Sauté the onion in a little bit of olive oil. Add the chili sauce, pineapple, lemon juice, brown sugar, Worcestershire sauce, ginger, and salt. Simmer for 15 minutes. Set aside.

Sprinkle the spare ribs with garlic powder and brown for 20 minutes.

Lower the temperature to 325°F and roast the ribs, basting often with the barbecue sauce, for another $1 1/2$ to 2 hours, or until the ribs are tender and falling off the bone.

Makes 6 servings

Cook's Tip

Cooking ribs in a crock-pot® keeps them tender and moist.

Critics' Comments

Spiced to perfection, this tangy sauce complements ribs, pork chops, or chicken. Hints of pineapple and ginger contribute to an outstanding flavor; it is a sauce that will challenge all competition.

—Peg and Marty Stout

Vidalia Onion Marmalade

From Anthony Jackson, a former student

1 1/2 pounds Vidalia onions, sliced
1/2 cup brown sugar, packed
1 stick salted butter
2/3 cup dry red wine
1/3 cup balsamic vinegar
3 tablespoons grenadine

Sauté the onions and brown sugar in the butter on medium heat until the onions are caramelized, 20 to 30 minutes, stirring occasionally.

Add the red wine, balsamic vinegar, and grenadine. Stirring constantly, reduce to a glaze, about 10 minutes. Serve with roasted or grilled meats, poultry, or fish.

Makes 2 cups

Italian Meat loaf

From Jamie Martin, a colleague

3 pounds ground beef
3 eggs
1/2 cup bread crumbs
Salt and pepper
1/4 pound prosciutto, sliced
1/4 pound provolone, sliced
1 cup green olives with pimento or garlic

Preheat the oven to 350°F.

Mix together the ground beef, eggs, bread crumbs, and salt and pepper.

Line a loaf pan with some of the prosciutto. Spread one third of the beef mixture into the loaf pan. Place half the provolone over the meat and top with half of the olives.

Arrange a couple of pieces of prosciutto over the olives and repeat the layers using half the remaining meat mixture, the rest of the provolone, and the olives, and half the remaining prosciutto.

Finish with the rest of the meat mixture and top with prosciutto. Bake for 1 1/2 to 2 hours, or until the meat loaf reaches an internal temperature of 170°F. Drain the fat and serve.

Makes 8–10 servings

Cook's Tips

A mixture of ground meats can be used, such as ground beef, pork, and veal.

Rinse the olives to reduce the saltiness.

Prosciutto adds an intense flavor to this meat loaf.

Lebanon bologna can be substituted for the prosciutto.

Corned Beef

From Sandra Piasecki, a colleague

The home technology department at Timberlane High School offers two programs. I teach foods and nutrition and Sandra Piasecki teaches child development. We have taught together for more than fifteen years and have developed a strong collegial relationship, always supporting each other's needs. During my early years at Timberlane, I found the district very demanding of its teachers. Sandi guided me through stressful times with a calm and reassuring approach. There was always someone telling us we couldn't do something, so Sandi and I would strategize to get what we wanted and not be discovered. We were successful 99 percent of the time.

As years passed by and I began to relax, the tides turned. I was now returning many of Sandi's words of wisdom. We have grown personally and professionally as a team. I could not have asked for a better friend and colleague.

 4 pounds corned beef brisket
 6 carrots, sliced on the slant
 1 medium onion, sliced thin
 1 cup sliced pitted prunes
 1 orange, sliced thin
 1 bay leaf
 2 tablespoons brown sugar, packed
 2 tablespoons honey
 1 tablespoon orange juice

Trim excess fat from the corned beef. Cover with cold water and soak for 1 hour.

Preheat the oven to 350°F.

GOOD FOOD SIMPLY PREPARED

Rinse the beef thoroughly and pat dry. Line a roasting pan with heavy-duty aluminum foil. Place the corned beef inside and top with vegetables and the prunes and orange slices. Add the bay leaf and cover tightly with foil. Bake for 3^1/$_2$ hours.

In a small bowl, combine the brown sugar, honey, and orange juice. Remove the foil covering the corned beef and brush the meat with the honey mixture. Bake 30 minutes more, or until the sugars caramelize.

Makes 8–10 servings

Cook's Tip

A plastic roasting bag can be used in place of aluminum foil.

St. Patrick's Day Gelatin Salad

From Ginny Karney, a colleague

1 small package (.3 ounce) lime Jell-O
1¼ cups boiling water
1 small onion, grated
½ cucumber, grated
1 pint cottage cheese
½ cup mayonnaise
½ cup blanched almonds, finely chopped

In a 6 cup casserole, dissolve the Jell-O in the boiling water; chill. When the Jell-O begins to thicken, stir in the remaining ingredients and chill in the refrigerator until solid. Cut into squares and serve on lettuce.

Makes 6 servings

Irish Soda Bread

From Sandra Piasecki, a colleague

3 cups flour
$^1/_2$ cup sugar
4 teaspoons baking powder
1 package (10 ounces) currants or raisins
$1^1/_2$ teaspoons salt
1 egg, lightly beaten
$1^1/_2$ cups milk
$^1/_4$ cup salted butter, melted

Preheat the oven to 350°F.

Mix together the flour, sugar, baking powder, currants, and salt in a large mixing bowl.

Stir in the egg, milk, and melted butter.

Pour the batter into a greased and floured 9 inch cake pan and bake for about 45 minutes. To test for doneness, insert a toothpick in the center. When it comes out clean, the soda bread is done.

Cook's Tip

Add 1 teaspoon of caraway seeds for a unique flavor.

Critic's Comments

This is truly like "coffee cake sweet bread"! The currants are so much better than plain raisins, too.

—Marilyn Prell

Raised Doughnuts

From Helen Willard, a colleague

1 cup shortening
1 cup boiling water
1/2 cup sugar
1 tablespoon salt
2 tablespoons yeast
1 cup lukewarm water
2 eggs, beaten
6 cups flour
Oil for frying
Powdered sugar for dusting

In a large bowl, mix together the shortening, boiling water, sugar, and salt. Stir until dissolved and let cool.

Dissolve the yeast in the 1 cup of lukewarm water. Mix into the cooled shortening mixture along with the eggs.

Stir in the flour. Chill the dough, covered, in the refrigerator at least 2 hours.

Roll out the dough 1/2 inch thick and cut with a doughnut cutter.

Let the cut doughnuts rise on a lightly floured board until double in size, about 30 minutes.

Deep-fry in oil at 350°F, topside down. Fry until the doughnuts are golden on both sides, about 1 minute each. Drain on paper towels. Serve plain or dust with powdered sugar.

Makes 2 dozen doughnuts

Cook's Tips

Roll doughnuts in granulated sugar or sugar with cinnamon mixed in.

Blend 1 cup of powdered sugar with 2 tablespoons of cream; add a drop of vanilla. Dip the doughnuts into the glaze and top with colored sprinkles.

Add 1 teaspoon of cocoa to the vanilla glaze to make chocolate.

Critic's Comments

If you love doughnuts, I don't imagine you'll ever buy another after experiencing these. Hot, moist, and decadent right out of the fryer, these doughnuts are sure to awaken taste buds you haven't used in years! Even after they cool, they are still unbelievably good. I have never enjoyed a doughnut like I enjoyed these. Make them. Your family will love you for it.

—Matt Morrison

Maple Walnut Bars

From Hugh Tonks, a colleague

Hugh Tonks was a member of the science department at Timberlane High for fifteen years. He was a graceful Englishman and I loved his accent. Hugh was diabetic and could not eat sweets, but his wife made these Maple Walnut Bars and sent them into school with Hugh to serve at various school functions. Hugh retired, but his recipe sure has not.

$1/2$ cup sugar
1 stick salted butter, softened
1 egg
2 teaspoons vanilla
1 cup rolled oats
1 cup walnuts, finely chopped
$2/3$ cup flour
$1/2$ cup pure maple syrup
$1/2$ teaspoon baking powder
$1/2$ teaspoon salt

Preheat the oven to 350°F.

Cream together the sugar and butter, in a large mixing bowl, until smooth.

Beat in the egg and vanilla.

Blend in the remaining ingredients.

Pour the batter into a greased and floured 9-inch square pan and bake for 30 to 35 minutes, or until the center springs back when

touched by your fingers. Cool to room temperature; cut into bars and serve.

Makes 9 bars

Cook's Tips

Cream the butter and sugar using the paddle attachment to an electric mixer. This beats in air that gives a nice texture.

Do not use instant oatmeal; it gives a mushy texture. Rolled oats are much healthier, as well.

Use Grade B dark amber maple syrup; it has a more pronounced maple flavor and seems less sweet.

Add to the batter $1/2$ teaspoon of cinnamon and/or $1/4$ teaspoon of nutmeg. Allspice and mace are good additions, too.

Critic's Comments

Moist and a bit crumbly, these pleasantly sweet bars are a perfect match with after-dinner coffee or a morning cup of Joe. Redolent with maple flavors, each nibble reminds me of my favorite pancake breakfast. After a cozy winter meal, maple bars are a great stand- alone dessert or delicious crumbled over ice cream. Hearty walnuts and oatmeal make these bars an ideal treat for before or after hiking. A super anytime indulgence!

—Maggie Simon

Pumpkin Cake

1½ cups sugar
4 eggs
¾ cup oil
2 cups pumpkin
2 teaspoons vanilla
2 cups flour
2 teaspoons baking soda
½ teaspoon salt
2 teaspoons cinnamon

Preheat the oven to 350°F.

Beat the sugar, eggs, and oil until thick and lemony.

Beat in the pumpkin and vanilla.

Stir in the flour, baking soda, salt, and cinnamon.

Pour the batter into a greased and floured 9-inch cake pan. Bake for 1½ hours, or until a knife inserted into the center of the cake comes out clean. Remove cake from pan and let cool.

Frost the cake with Cream Cheese Frosting, below.

Makes 12 servings

Cream Cheese Frosting
3 ounces cream cheese, at room temperature
$1/2$ stick salted butter, softened
$6^1/2$ cups confectioner's sugar
1 tablespoon milk
$1/2$ teaspoon vanilla

Beat the cream cheese and butter for several minutes, until completely smooth. Beat in the remaining ingredients until the consistency is spreadable.

Apple Blondies

From Joanne Cook, a colleague

1 stick salted butter, melted
1/2 cup sugar
1 egg
1 teaspoon vanilla
2 cups chopped apples
1 cup flour
1/2 teaspoon cinnamon
1/2 teaspoon baking powder
1/2 teaspoon baking soda

Preheat the oven to 350°F.

Beat the butter and sugar.

Beat in the egg and vanilla.

Stir in the remaining ingredients. Pour into a greased and floured 8-inch square cake pan. Bake for 30 to 35 minutes, or until the top springs back when touched by your fingers. Cool; then dust with confectioner's sugar and cut into bars.

Makes 9 bars

The Best Blueberry Scones

From Patty Williams, a colleague

When I'm out of school for a day, I don't trust my kitchen to just any substitute teacher; Patty Williams is an exception. Our styles of teaching and discipline are similar, and I have always felt comfortable leaving my classroom and students under Patty's command.

What is extra special is that Patty likes doing her own lesson plans using her own recipes. My students raved about her recipe for scones, and I have added it to my cookbook of ultimate favorites. Simple to make, these are moist and bursting with fruit.

$^2/_3$ cup salted butter
$^3/_4$ cup sugar
1 egg
1 teaspoon vanilla or almond extract
3 cups flour
1 tablespoon baking powder
1 teaspoon salt
$^1/_4$ teaspoon baking soda
$^3/_4$ cup milk
1 cup blueberries
1 cup chopped walnuts

Preheat the oven to 400°F.

Beat the butter until it is soft and smooth. Beat in the sugar. Beat in the egg and vanilla.

In a large mixing bowl, combine the flour, baking soda, salt, and baking powder and blend well. Add alternately with the milk, in three additions, to the butter mixture.

Stir in the berries and nuts.

Using an ice-cream scoop, drop the dough onto a greased sheet pan and bake for 15 minutes, or until the tops springs bake when touched by your fingers. Let cool and then glaze.

Glaze
4 tablespoons confectioner's sugar
4 teaspoons fresh lemon juice

Whisk together the sugar and lemon juice. Dip the tops of the scones into the glaze.

Cook's Tips

Always use butter in baking; margarine is an unhealthy trans-fat.

Add 2 teaspoons of grated orange or lemon rind for a nice tang; fresh is better, but dried rind is fine, too.

Use any kind of nuts: walnuts, pecans, almonds, or filberts. Nuts have healthy fats.

Use different berries: blueberries, cranberries, raspberries, or currants, for example. Freeze before adding them to the batter; they will retain their shape better.

Don't overbeat the dough or the scones will be too tough.

Critics' Comments

A blend of butter, flour, and sugar, these scones are perfectly textured and baked so that they are moist yet light. Walnut chunks and vanilla flavoring enhance the taste of the juicy blueberries. Whether they are served warm from the oven or at room temperature with tea or coffee, the consensus is that these are *the* best scones anyone has ever tasted.

—Peg and Marty Stout

CHAPTER SIX

Summers in Maine

Summers in Maine

My love of summers in Maine began when I was five years old. During Dad's two-week vacation, my parents rented an old lodge that had been converted into a camp on Rangeley Lake. The entire Styrna family was there: Baba and Grandpa; Mom and Dad; my sister, Christine, and I; my aunt Beverly and uncle Ed; and cousins Sandy and Susan.

This was my initiation to long summer days of swimming and playing in the clean, clear waters of a Maine lake. My cousins and I were in the lake from morning until night, coming out only when our lips were blue and our mothers insisted. We lived the ideal life for children there—freedom to swim, play, eat, and sleep when we wanted, under the somewhat watchful eyes of our parents, who also were living the ideal life for two weeks.

There were many first experiences on this vacation, but one of my most memorable ones was my first lobster. The lobsterman wrote my name on the lobster claw and I easily recognized it when it came out of the steam pit. I still remember loving the taste of the meat from the claw, tail, and body.

For the next three years we rented a little log cabin on the shores of Belgrade Lake. It was here that Dad introduced me to fishing, using Grandpa's old bamboo poles. We would wake at five in the morning, row out into the lake several hundred feet, and drop anchor. Dad had the pleasure of baiting the hook while I sat, watched, and waited for the cork attached to the line to be pulled underwater, a sign that there was a fish. Reacting with excitement, I always screamed and cried. Each time I waited impatiently for Dad to remove the fish, bait the hook, and get it back into the water again. We often caught small white perch, enough for a supper or two.

One summer we spent our vacation by the ocean at a lovely cottage on Spruce Head Island. The ocean's edge was a new playground for me. There were little creatures hiding in the fish pools when the tide went out. Living under the seaweed were periwinkles, barnacles, ocean mussels, starfish, and sea urchins; they

became my friends. Frequently, large pink jellyfish washed ashore and I threw rocks at them, watching their jelly splat all around. The foghorn at the lighthouse on the other side of the island usually awakened us at night with its loud haunting sound, somewhat daunting at first, but comforting as we came to recognize it.

One of our great memories of that cottage is when Uncle Ed and Dad went into a nearby cove and dug clams, which were soaked in ocean water and cleansed naturally of sand. At the cottage, Aunt Beverly steamed them in beer and then she and my uncle enjoyed every one. Neither of my parents, my sister, or I could bring our-selves to try "the slimy-looking things." I must admit that this ini-tial impression has changed dramatically over the years, as today we all enjoy clams steamed, fried, stuffed, and baked.

We finally ended up at a camp on Swan Lake, and it was there that we heard of a somewhat rundown camp being sold by an eld-erly couple who could no longer enjoy and care for it. On Columbus Day weekend in 1964 we purchased the sixty-year-old camp, with its musty smell, from Arthur and Sara Guthrie. The following spring we went to work making the camp ours, airing it out and cleaning up years of cobwebs and mouse droppings.

Typically, when a Maine camp changes hands, it is sold full of furnishings, including dishes, linens, and trinkets. Our camp was no exception. It was filled with antiques. The kitchen had a cast-iron sink and a Hoosier food pantry with a pullout counter, flour bin, and cabinets to store baking equipment and supplies. In the corner was a built-in china cabinet filled with multicolored Luray dishes dating from the early forties. There was a three-burner electric stove with an oven to its side and a woodstove for heat. Over the years we have updated the very old kitchen, making cooking easier and more pleasurable.

The focal point in the living room is a beautiful fireplace made from stones collected along the shoreline of the lake. Next to the fireplace off in a corner are built-in bookshelves full of novels and *Reader's Digest*s dating back to the 1920s. On one of the shelves, we found Sara Guthrie's wooden recipe box. Her hand-written

recipes include a simple list of ingredients with measurements described as a shake of this and a mug of that and instructions to bake in a moderately hot oven; no temperatures or exact measurements are given. We have added our own recipes to Sara's heirloom recipe box, and although I have never tried any of Sara's recipes, I enjoy browsing through them every summer.

On the lake side of the camp is a big screened-in porch the width of the camp where we have sat for hours mesmerized by the lake, with views of a range of mountains in the background, and spectacular sunsets. We watch families of ducks and loons raise their young while they keep an eye on the eagles above. We have seen deer swimming across the lake as well as an occasional moose wading at daybreak. There have also been sightings of bears, foxes, fishers, partridges, and coyotes. Fishing is a peaceful activity, as are boating and kayaking. A spring-fed lake, the water is so pristine that bathing is cool and refreshing.

Our two-week vacations in Maine have now been extended to whole summers; we usually arrive in early June and stay until late September. This has given us opportunities to explore many facets of Maine life.

A particular favorite place is Moosehead Lake, in Greenville. We have always taken the same route to the lake, along the Kennebec River, because we love the first impressive sight of Moosehead's Mount Keneo. Traveling along the west side, we stop at Wilson dam to watch the fishermen catch jumbo salmon or stop for a tram ride up Squaw Mountain to see breathtaking views of Moosehead Lake. After a boat ride on the lake or an airplane ride over the Allagash searching for forest fires and wildlife, we settle in comfortably at the Greenville Inn and enjoy a sumptuous meal. Early the next morning, we head north along Lily Bay to Kokadjo and the Golden Road, where you can drive for miles and see no one except for an occasional logging truck. Moose and bear sometimes cross the road, and their presence is always admired but always respected as well. Our wilderness getaway usually concludes with a picnic in Baxter State Park, with Mount Katahdin looming in the background.

One summer, Dad and I made reservations to stay at a cabin on Daicey Pond in Baxter State Park, where we wanted to do some hiking along the Appalachian Trail and around the pond. This was our first adventure into true wilderness: no electricity, stove, refrigeration, running water, or bathroom! My greatest concern was meals. Experienced campers were recommending dry goods and prepackaged trail meals, but that was unappealing and I was determined to eat gourmet in the wilderness. We planned our menus ahead of time, preparing and freezing baked stuffed haddock with clams and filet mignon. Fresh vegetables were precut, garnished with herbs and olive oil, and wrapped tightly in foil. A cold chest was packed with lots of ice with our frozen foods buried; the vegetables were placed on top to keep cold.

Our food defrosted slowly, but in time to be cooked on a table-size kettle grill, which we had brought with us and placed on a picnic table outside our cabin. For breakfast we ate bacon sautéed in a pan on the grill, scrambled eggs in bacon fat, bread toasted over the open coals, and fresh coffee brewed on the grill in an old coffeepot, timed by instinct. Neighboring campers were drawn to our picnic table by the aromas of obvious gourmet food in this rustic setting. Knowing we were amateurs in the wilderness, a ranger had questioned our ability to survive, but after taking note of a couple of our meals, he determined we were quite capable.

Another favorite getaway is Bar Harbor, and we have discovered that June is the best month, before the tourists infiltrate, to explore that area. From a drive up Cadillac Mountain, the views over Bar Harbor and Frenchmen's Bay are unparalleled. We might spend time watching the Bluenose ferry depart to Nova Scotia, enjoying the hiking around Jordan Pond, casually driving along Somes Sound—the only fjord in America—and dining on a seafood feast at Thurston's Pound overlooking a lobstermen's harbor.

Summer is never complete without a gourmet picnic at Schoodic Point. Traveling to Gouldsboro, we stop at Bartlett's winery for a couple of bottles of wine. Driving down the peninsula, we stop at Schoodic Point to admire the vast ocean view with fiery waves

crashing over the rocks. Our particular picnic spot is a very private ledge looking north on the Maine coast. With binoculars, we watch lobstermen ride from buoy to buoy checking their catch as a flock of seagulls follows close behind. Sips of apple blush wine are followed by bites of smoked trout pâté, smoked oysters, smoked salmon wrapped around wedges of melon, crusty rye bread spread with champagne mustard and garnished with duck pâté or salami, and crudités such as red peppers, grape tomatoes, cucumbers, and green olives: truly a royal feast.

One of my most memorable times was spent with my father on Monhegan Island. On this three-day excursion, we spent the first day at an inn in Tenants Harbor, sitting, talking, and enjoying the serenity. Our plans were to ride the ferry to the island, check in at the inn, and spend a casual day strolling around. Before leaving Tenants Harbor we picked up a wedge of cheese, a bunch of grapes, and a bottle of water for a picnic along the trails on Monhegan. The site approaching Monhegan Island looked like a Norman Rockwell painting, so picturesque!

I was eager to explore the island, but as we began our afternoon stroll, it wasn't long before I realized that the trails on the island were beyond strolling. My breaths were deepening and my strides shortening. As we approached the farthest side of the island, we descended a sharp slope and stopped on a ledge about two hundred feet above the ocean, with frightening waves crashing on the ledges. I was panicking when an elderly, white-haired woman using walking sticks casually approached up to us. She recognized our fear and told us that in her younger years at age sixty—she wanted to be walking these trails when she was ninety, refusing to spend time in a nursing home. With her encouragement, we proceeded with our challenging hike up steep trails and down steep trails, resting often.

We put aside the salt-laden cheese and rationed what little water and grapes we had. We proudly returned to our inn exhausted and dehydrated, and after a home-cooked meal and a good night's sleep, we began another day of hiking. We often think back to this experience and the wisdom of the old woman.

I live for summers at Swan Lake. I enjoy nature walks up the road looking for wildlife and wildflowers. I love listening to the loons and other birds, feeling the wind across my face, the fresh air, sea breezes, and ocean fog. I tend to a woodland garden of hosta, trillium, and jack-in-the-pulpit and an herb garden filled with chives, sage, oregano, dill, parsley, and thyme, which I use to cook with organic foods purchased from local farmer's markets.

This little camp on Swan Lake is a place in the country I go in order to reconnect with my soul; it is my sanctuary, a place where my creativity in cooking is rekindled each year. It was a sad day I'm sure for Arthur and Sara Guthrie when they sold their camp to my parents, but four decades later we still love and care for their cherished camp.

Crabmeat Dip

Fresh crabmeat is readily available along the coast of Maine. During the summer months, when friends and family get together, someone always makes crabmeat dip. People's recipes are similar, with just slight variations.

8 ounces cream cheese
1 pound fresh Maine crabmeat
1 tablespoon horseradish
1 teaspoon fresh lemon juice
$1/2$ teaspoon Rooster sauce or 4 drops Tabasco
Paprika
Parmesan cheese

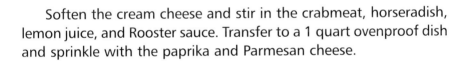

Preheat the oven to 375°F.

Soften the cream cheese and stir in the crabmeat, horseradish, lemon juice, and Rooster sauce. Transfer to a 1 quart ovenproof dish and sprinkle with the paprika and Parmesan cheese.

Bake for 15 to 20 minutes, or until the cheese is bubbling. Serve with crackers or chips.

Makes 3 cups

Cook's Tips

Rooster sauce, known as Asian ketchup, is a flavorful, medium-hot sauce found in Asian markets.

Mix fresh crabmeat with mayonnaise and hot sauce for another simple dip and serve with chips or crackers.

Any dish is as good as the quality of its ingredients.

Smoked Salmon Pâté

I made this recipe for years using cream cheese. I started experimenting with tofu for health reasons and this recipe adapted itself
beautifully. Tofu has no flavor of its own; it picks up flavors from
other foods, so use a heavy hand when measuring the flavoring
ingredients. My sister told me not to try any of my tofu recipes on
her because she wouldn't eat them. I secretly served this pâté as an
hors d'oeuvre on Christmas Day and Chris consumed crackerful after
crackerful.

3/4 pound tofu or cream cheese
4 ounces smoked salmon
1–2 tablespoons horseradish
1 tablespoon fresh lemon juice
1 tablespoon minced chives
2 teaspoons grated onion
1 teaspoon dill
3/4 teaspoon salt
1/2 teaspoon pepper

Blend all the ingredients in the food processor. Refrigerate several hours. Serve on crackers or small rye bread rounds.

Makes 3 cups

Cook's Tip

For an even more elegant pâté, garnish with a sliver of smoked
salmon and some caviar.

Benedictine

Throughout the years, our neighbors on Swan Lake have gotten together for various social hours. Maggie Simon makes a delicious sandwich spread that is popular in her home state of Kentucky. I always look forward to a luncheon for the ladies hosted by Maggie and her aunt Kathy on the porch of Sunnyside, their cottage overlooking Swan Lake, where Benedictine can be expected.

1 pound cream cheese
1 medium cucumber
1 small onion, grated
1 teaspoon salt
Dash Tabasco
Mayonnaise
2–3 drops of green food coloring

Beat the cream cheese until it is soft and smooth.

Peel and seed the cucumber. Grate the pulp; wrap the pulp in cheesecloth and squeeze until it is fairly dry. Add the cucumber to the cream cheese along with the onion, salt, and Tabasco.

Add mayonnaise until the Benedictine is of a nice, spreadable consistency. Add food coloring to give a slight green tinge.

Spread the Benedictine on sandwich bread, crusts removed, and cut into diamonds. Serve as an hors d'oeuvre.

Makes 3 cups

Peppered Smoked Trout Pâté

The food in Maine always tastes so good. Dad says it's because of the clean air and unpolluted soil and waters.

Duck Trap River Smokehouse in Belfast, Maine, takes seafood from the cold ocean waters and smokes it to perfection. The original smokehouse was an adorable log cabin located along the Duck Trap River. The smokehouse is now housed in a large industrial building. Duck Trap makes wonderful smoked seafood pâtés. One time while we were visiting the smokehouse, they were experimenting with a recipe for peppered smoked trout pâté that I thought was fabulous. The peppered pâté was never marketed, so I tried making it on my own: This is the result.

3/4 pound firm tofu
4 ounces Duck Trap peppered smoked trout
1–2 tablespoons horseradish
1 tablespoon fresh lemon juice
2 teaspoons grated onion
3/4 teaspoon salt
1/2 teaspoon pepper

Put all the ingredients in a food processor and process until smooth. Adjust the seasonings and refrigerate for several hours, until firm. Serve on crackers or use as a dip.

Makes 3 cups

Cook's Tips

Regular, light, or fat-free cream cheese can be used in place of the tofu.

Serve with crusty bread, crackers, chips, or vegetables.

Critics' Comments

Perfect for an appetizer before dinner or as a lunch, this pâté is light and smooth with a smoky taste. A little kick of horseradish gives it a spicy bite; a hint of lemon is refreshing. A secret ingredient gives it body and protein but no fat!

—Peg and Marty Stout

Fourth of July at Swan Lake
Clam Chowder

Being from New England and raised on clam chowder, I am a big fan, and I have yet to find chowder that equals this one. I make it with freshly dug Maine littleneck clams. It is a Fourth of July dinner tradition.

We buy 15 pounds of clams, steam them, and shuck them at the kitchen table with pails and bibs, reserving their briny broth for the chowder. New baby red potatoes just beginning to come out of the ground adds to the authenticity of the chowder. Friends of ours, Dave and Tatianna Leach, have joined us for a couple of celebrations. They have since retired to Arizona, and say they wish there was a "clam chowder pipeline" across the country to satisfy their cravings.

2 cups water
15 pounds Littleneck clams
1 cup diced onion
1 cup diced celery
1 cup diced green pepper
1 stick salted butter or olive oil, but butter is better
2 teaspoons ground thyme
1 1/2 teaspoons curry powder
1/2 cup flour
1 heaping quart diced potatoes
1 can (12 ounces) evaporated milk
Salt and pepper

In a deep pot, bring the water to a boil. Add the clams, cover, and steam until the shells have opened, 8 to 12 minutes depending on their size.

Remove the clams from the pot and cool slightly. Shell the clams and pull the black skin off their necks. Reserve the clams (about 1 quart). Strain the clam broth (about 2 quarts) through several layers of cheesecloth and set aside.

Sauté the onion, celery, and green pepper in the butter until soft. Add the thyme and curry powder and sauté a bit longer. Mix in the flour to form a roux.

Whisk in the clam broth and bring to a boil, stirring constantly. Add the potatoes and simmer until the potatoes are soft, about 30 minutes.

Stir in the reserved clams and the evaporated milk. Heat through. Season with salt and pepper.

Makes 4 quarts

Cook's Tips

Butter and cream always taste better, but a healthier alternative is olive oil and evaporated milk. You choose!

Buy your clams from a reputable fish market that gets its clams from a reliable source. In Maine, I buy my clams from Young's Lobster Pound in Belfast. They keep their clams in ocean water, where they naturally clean themselves of sand. Dad and I take the ice cooler to the pound to transport the clams; Mom has the cooking pots awaiting our return. After the clams are steamed, strain the clam broth through several layers of cheesecloth or coffee filters to remove any leftover sand.

Curry powder is the secret ingredient here. Don't omit it. Herbs and spices should enhance a dish, not take over.

Critics' Comments

An alternative to the traditional cream-based New England clam chowder, this one has a subtle flavor of curry that enhances the overall impression of unique chowder. There's a nice blend of ingredients with small chunks of potato complementing the whole clams, which produce the dominant flavor. Delicious! Succulent! Zesty!

—Peg and Marty Stout

Cold Beet Soup

1 pound beets, with the greens
6¹/₂ cups cold water
3 tablespoons red wine vinegar
5 teaspoons salt
1¹/₂ teaspoons sugar
4 scallions
2 cucumbers
1 cup sour cream
4 tablespoons fresh dill
3 tablespoons lemon juice
2 teaspoons pepper

Peel the beets and cut into a thin julienne. Wash the leaves and cut into thin shreds. Cover the beets and greens with the cold water, then add the vinegar, salt, and sugar. Simmer until the beets are cooked, about 30 minutes. Set aside to cool.

Cut the scallions into thin rounds. Peel the cucumbers and cut into small chunks. Add to the beets.

Stir in the sour cream, dill, lemon juice, and pepper. Taste and adjust the seasonings.

Makes 3 quarts

Zucchini Pancakes

I am in heaven when the farmer's markets open and fresh produce comes in season. The taste is beyond anything frozen or canned.

3 medium zucchini
3 large potatoes
3 cloves garlic
1 large sweet onion
1 egg
1 tablespoon salt
$1^1/_2$ teaspoons pepper
$^1/_4$ teaspoon nutmeg
$^1/_2$–$^3/_4$ cup flour
Olive oil for frying

Using the grater attachment to the food processor, grate the zucchini. Transfer to a large mixing bowl.

Using the blade attachment, puree the potatoes, garlic, and onion. Stir into the zucchini.

Stir in the egg, salt, pepper, and nutmeg. Add enough flour (start with $^1/_2$ cup) to absorb the excess moisture.

Add a film of oil to a moderately hot frying pan. Pour in the batter, $1/4$ cup at a time, and cook pancakes until golden, about 8 minutes on each side.

Makes 24 pancakes

Cook's Tips

Add more flour to the batter as needed to absorb excess water from the zucchini and potatoes.

Be creative and use other vegetables in place of or in addition to the zucchini, such as yellow squash, spinach, and carrots.

Experiment with flavors by adding herbs and spices such as dill or curry.

Bagaduce Falls Potato Teasers

Every summer we take a field trip to Bagaduce Falls and treat ourselves to a Maine fried seafood dinner. We always order fried clams, fried haddock, and "potato teasers," delicious puffs of shredded potatoes stuffed with a peppery cheese, then breaded and deep-fried. Dad and I carry our tray overflowing with specialties to a picnic table, where Mom awaits patiently along the falls. We marvel over the scenery as we aggressively down our meal. Frequently there are kayakers navigating the falls, eagles soaring high above (probably eyeing our lunch), and seagulls waiting for any leftovers. The owner's dog waits gracefully for any treats, too.

After lunch we take a walk to admire the beautiful daylilies and tiger lilies that grow along the edge of Bagaduce Falls. Leaving the falls with an ice-cream cone—caramel caribou is my favorite—we drive leisurely around the peninsula enjoying the scenery.

My students enthusiastically make potato teasers year after year. They prefer deep-frying for a crispier outside and eating them with ketchup or sour cream, but at home I sauté them in olive oil for a healthier result.

This is my adaptation of Potato Teasers. I make them with cold leftover mashed potatoes. They are quite different, and can be served as a side dish or appetizer.

5 pounds Yukon gold potatoes
$1/2$ bay leaf
$1/2$ stick salted butter
1 cup evaporated milk
$1/8$ teaspoon nutmeg
Salt and pepper
Pepper Jack cheese or Velveeta, cut into small wedges
1 cup flour, seasoned with salt and pepper
2 eggs, beaten

1 cup plain or seasoned bread crumbs

Peel, quarter, and boil the potatoes with the bay leaf until soft. Drain and discard the bay leaf. Mash the potatoes with the butter and evaporated milk. Season with the nutmeg, salt, and pepper. Chill overnight.

Take some mashed potatoes the size of a golf ball in the palm of your hand. Sink a wedge of cheese into the center, making sure that all the cheese is covered with the potatoes. Dredge the potato balls in flour, dip in the beaten eggs, and roll in the bread crumbs. Deep-fry at 350°F until deep golden brown, about 3 minutes.

Makes 35 puffs

Cook's Tips

Yukon gold make a terrific mashed potato, and they are readily available.

Adding a half a bay leaf to the potato-boiling water adds a subtle flavor.

Never use margarine; it is an unhealthy transfat. Butter is better and more flavorful. Olive oil is even better.

I like canned evaporated milk: it's creamy without the fat of cream.

Nutmeg is another secret ingredient in making mashed potatoes.

Always season foods with salt and pepper to taste. There is no measuring here.

I use peanut oil for deep-frying, a healthy oil that adds flavor.

Be sure the cheese is sealed within the mashed potato. Otherwise, it will leak during frying and make a mess.

Critics' Comments

These puffs, crispy on the outside with a cheesy center, bring life and zest to the potato. Lightly seasoned Yukon gold potatoes are complemented, but not overwhelmed, by the spiciness of a pepper cheese. Dip these tasty morsels in your everyday ketchup or a spicy hot sauce and you'll find it difficult to eat just a few.

—Peg and Marty Stout

Maxim's Potatoes

For the past two decades we have left Maine for the summer season on Columbus Day weekend with 500 pounds of Maxim's potatoes from Thorndike, Maine. Maxim's grows Norwich potatoes, an all-purpose potato. They are "field run," which means out of the ground as is: small, medium, and quite large. We look forward to the foliage as we drive through the back roads of Maine to get these potatoes. The earthy smell in the barn reflects newly dug potatoes and fills us with anticipation for crispy baked potatoes for supper that night, not to mention the many potato dishes for the winter evenings to come.

The potatoes are stored in big bins that are measured out into barrels and sold to the locals for an extremely reasonable price. The potatoes are untreated, the dirt still clinging to them. The Norwich is what a potato is supposed to taste like. There have been many years when the potatoes were dug the day before the Columbus Day weekend and we brought them home and laid them out on the garage floor with fans blowing to dry them before winter storage.

Every Columbus Day we say to the potato farmer, "See you next year, if God willing."

Summer Vegetable Juice

In September, when vegetables are abundant, I like to make juice from fresh produce from the farmer's market. Canned into Mason jars, my family has juice all winter long.

1/2 bushel tomatoes, cored
1 bunch celery
4 carrots, peeled
4 cloves garlic, peeled
2 large sweet onions, peeled
2 red sweet peppers, seeded
2 tablespoons dry mustard
2 tablespoons salt
2 tablespoons sugar
1/4 teaspoon cayenne

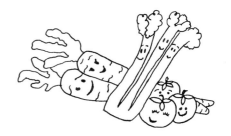

Juice the vegetables following the manufacturer's directions for your juice machine. Season the juice with the dry mustard, salt, sugar, and cayenne. Bring the juice to a boil, can, and process.

Cook's Tips

Store juice at room temperature for up to a year.

I use a Vita Mix food processor to puree the vegetables; it makes juice out of the skins of the vegetables, which add healthy fiber.

Substitute jalapeño peppers for the red sweet peppers if you like more spice.

Add 1 pound of spinach leaves or a bunch of parsley leaves.

Corn, Tomato, and Avocado Salsa

The families in my neighborhood keep in touch with various social gatherings throughout the year. Such activities are a winter bonfire with a midwestern pork barbecue, a Sunday brunch, a pig roast, and southern deep-fried turkey, to name a few themes.

One summer my friend Audrey brought the neighbors together when her son Erich came home after a ten-year stay in Nepal. He is a world traveler and gourmet cook. Erich brought a few of his friends and prepared a barbecue of marinated pork loin, spinach salad, potato salad, and a corn salad with avocados and tomatoes. It was one of the best meals I have ever had. It was simple, healthful, flavorful, and perfectly prepared. I fell in love with the corn salad, studied the ingredients, and memorized the flavors. This is my recollection.

1/4 cup red wine vinegar
2 teaspoons mustard
1 teaspoon minced garlic
1/2 teaspoon salt
1/4 teaspoon pepper
1/2 cup olive oil
8 ears corn
4 avocados, diced
4 large tomatoes, diced
1 large sweet onion, diced
1/3 cup chopped parsley
Salt and pepper

Combine the vinegar, mustard, garlic, salt, and pepper. Slowly whisk in the olive oil and let stand several hours to blend the flavors.

Husk the corn and cut the kernels off the cob. Cook the corn in a sauté pan with about a 1/4 cup of water until the kernels are almost dry, about 5 minutes.

Put the corn in a bowl with the avocados, tomatoes, onion, and parsley. Toss with the dressing; season with salt and pepper.

Makes 8 servings

Cook's Tips

This is a great summer salad when all the ingredients are fresh from the local farmer.

Use good-quality vinegars; they really make a difference.

Dissolve the salt in vinegar before adding the oil. Salt will not dissolve in oil.

I use a lot of garlic, so I peel and chop several heads and store them in a considerable amount of olive oil in the refrigerator. That way, garlic is ready when I am.

Use a good-quality olive oil from Spain, Greece, or Italy for salad dressings and dipping bread.

Hass avocados have a wrinkled skin; they are creamier and more flavorful than others.

When using onions raw, choose a sweet onion variety that is milder with a bit more natural sugar than the cooking onions.

Always use fresh parsley; dried parsley has no flavor.

Critics' Comments

A perfectly seasoned combination of vegetables featuring fresh corn as the dominant ingredient. This unique side dish lends a degree of lightness to an evening meal on a hot summer night.

—Peg and Marty Stout

Russian Rye Bread

1 tablespoon yeast
$^1/_2$ teaspoon sugar
$1^1/_2$ cups water
1 ounce unsweetened chocolate
2 tablespoons instant coffee granules
1 tablespoon molasses
1 tablespoon salt
$^1/_4$ cup oil
$^1/_2$ cup boiling water
2 cups rye flour
5–6 cups bread flour
2 tablespoons caraway seeds
2 tablespoons flaxseeds

Dissolve the yeast and sugar in the $1^1/_2$ cups water and set aside for 10 minutes. The yeast will proof and turn bubbly, yielding a characteristic aroma.

Dissolve the chocolate, instant coffee, molasses, salt, and oil in the boiling water and set aside.

When the yeast mixture is bubbly, add the rye flour, 4 cups of bread flour, caraway seed, and flaxseeds. Pour in the chocolate mixture and begin to stir the ingredients until a ball of dough forms, about 2 minutes.

Knead the dough for 10 minutes, incorporating the last cup of flour as needed to make a soft dough that does not stick to your hands. Place the dough in a bowl, cover with plastic wrap, and allow it to rise until it is double in bulk, 2 to 4 hours, depending on the temperature of the room.

Preheat the oven to 375°F.

Punch down the dough and knead a few times. Shape the bread and allow to rise again until double in bulk, about 2 hours. Bake on a stone in the oven for 1 hour, or until the loaf sounds hollow when tapped. Cool on a rack.

Makes 1 large or 2 small loaves

Cook's Tips

Purée a large sweet onion and add to the dough. It imparts a pleasant sweet taste and provides food for the yeast in the form of sugar.

Use bread flour, as it contains more gluten, which helps in the rising and structure of the dough.

I use a heavy hand when measuring the caraway and flaxseeds; they intensify the flavor of the baked bread.

Breads produce great taste when allowed to rise slowly. Make the dough in the evening and let rise overnight at a cool room temperature, 55 to 60 degrees.

Preheat a baking stone in the oven and bake the bread directly on the stone to produce a European-style crusty loaf.

Use a baker's peel sprinkled with cornmeal to move the bread onto and take it off the stone. The cornmeal prevents sticking and adds flavor to the bread.

Slash the top of the dough before it goes into the oven. This allows for greater rising and expansion.

Let bread dough rise in breadbaskets made in Austria specifically for the purpose. These produce authentic- and attractive-looking loaves.

Spritz the oven several times with water while the bread is baking to enhance a crusty loaf.

Allow freshly baked bread to cool a bit before you slice, as the bread will turn gummy.

This bread freezes well.

Critic's Comments

Nothing makes a dreary day into a sunny one better than homemade bread. On a gray, gloomy day, this magnificent double loaf arrived in our cottage kitchen still warm from the oven. Sliced and buttered, the bread was a meal in itself. Minutes later, the bread proved ideal for sandwiches. When it cooled, we sliced it, drizzled olive oil over the slices, and grilled them as a dinner accompaniment. As is the case with all dark breads, this loaf was dense in texture and earthy in color—easy to slice and tasty enough to eat without any accompaniment.

All of us declared this recipe perfect. The loaf presented to us was a double loaf—had it been just my husband and me, finishing the loaf in a timely fashion would have been a daunting task. We were fortunate in that we had company, and the bread became a centerpiece at two dinner parties. Making two loaves might be a better idea for small families.

—Barbara Simon

Rye Bread

One summer I took a workshop on European bread baking at the Culinary Institute of America in New York. I brought home approximately twenty different loaves of bread that I had learned how to make. My family loved these hearty breads and since then we make our own using recipes we adapted from that workshop.

Our neighbors on Swan Lake look forward to the aroma and taste of the fresh bread we make on an almost daily basis. Three of our favorite bread recipes are here.

1 tablespoon brown sugar
1 tablespoon yeast
2 cups warm water
4 cups bread flour
2 cups rye flour
2 tablespoons caraway seeds
2 tablespoons golden flax seeds
1 tablespoon molasses
1 tablespoon oil
1 tablespoon salt
1 onion, finely sliced

In a large mixing bowl, dissolve the brown sugar and yeast in the warm water. Let rest until bubbly, about 10 minutes.

Add the remaining ingredients in the order listed and begin to stir them until a ball of dough forms. Knead the dough for 10 minutes, incorporating flour as needed to make a soft dough that does not stick to your hands.

Put the dough in a bowl, cover with plastic wrap, and let rest until double in bulk, 2 to 4 hours, depending on the temperature of the room.

Punch down the dough, shape the bread, and allow it to rise again until double in bulk, about 2 hours.

Preheat the oven to 375°F. Insert a stone slab to preheat as well.

Bake on the stone for 1 hour, or until the loaf sounds hollow when tapped. Cool on a rack.

Makes 1 large or 2 small loaves

Cook's Tips

Replace the sliced onion with 2 cups of sauerkraut. Do not omit the onion or sauerkraut, as it provides food for the yeast and creates great flavor.

If using the dough hook to an electric mixer, knead on number 2 for 2 minutes, then knead on number 4 for 8 minutes.

Refer to Cook's Tips for Russian Rye Bread (page 225).

GOOD FOOD SIMPLY PREPARED

Cheese Bread

1 tablespoon sugar
1 tablespoons dry yeast
2 cups water
5–6 cups bread flour
2 cups sharp Cheddar cheese, grated
$\frac{1}{4}$ cup Parmesan cheese, grated
1 tablespoon salt
2 teaspoons dry mustard
$\frac{1}{8}$ teaspoon cayenne pepper

In a large mixing bowl, dissolve the sugar and yeast in the water and set aside for 10 minutes. The yeast will proof and turn bubbly, yielding a characteristic aroma.

Add 5 cups of flour and the remaining ingredients and begin to stir together until a ball of dough forms.

Knead the dough for 10 minutes, incorporating the last cup of flour as needed to make a soft dough that does not stick to your hands. Put the dough in a bowl, cover with plastic wrap, and allow it to rise until double in bulk, 2 to 4 hours, depending on the temperature of the room.

Punch down the dough and knead a few times. Shape the bread, put it in a buttered loaf pan and allow it to rise again until double in bulk, about 2 hours.

Preheat the oven to 375°F.

Bake for 1 hour, or until the loaf sounds hollow when tapped.

Makes 1 loaf

Cook's Tip

This bread makes great French toast.

Blackberry Custard Torte

Peggy and Marty Stout have been our next-door neighbors on Swan Lake for the past thirty years. We have many interests in common, including hiking around Moosehead Lake, Monhegan Island, and Baxter State Park; lobster and steamed clams; evening meals on the front porch; sunsets; and wildlife. We eagerly anticipate summer, when we will share our stories and experiences.

One summer the blackberries were abundant around the lake. My family picked and froze 55 quarts of berries for winter enjoyment. Peggy gave me this recipe, which she got from a local pastry chef, to help us utilize our blackberry supply.

Dough
 1 cup flour
 $1/2$ cup sugar
 $1 1/2$ teaspoons baking powder
 1 stick cold, salted butter cut into cubes
 1 egg
 2 cups fresh blackberries

To make the dough, place the flour, sugar, baking powder, and butter in a food processor and process until crumbly. Add the egg and process briefly until a dough forms on top of the blade. Wrap the dough in plastic wrap and refrigerate for 30 minutes.

Using your fingertips, spread the dough into the bottom and $1/2$ inch up the sides of a 9-inch spring-form pan. Spread the blackberries evenly on top of the dough.

Topping

    2 cups sour cream
    $1/2$ cup sugar
    2 yolks
    $1/2$ teaspoon cinnamon

Preheat the oven to 350°F.

Whisk together the topping ingredients and pour over the berries. Bake for 40 to 50 minutes, or until set. Let torte cool. Serve with whipped cream and more berries.

Makes 8 servings

Cooks Tip

Substitute fresh blueberries or raspberries for the blackberries.

Critic's Comments

My husband said, "This one's a keeper!" The creamy, custard-like texture contrasted with the crunchiness of the berries for a delightful burst in my mouth. What a surprise to discover the bottom to be cookie dough instead of the usual piecrust. The pale purple color looked beautiful against my white china, too.

—Marilyn Prell

Raspberry Shortcake Cookies

During the summer months, I browse through farmer's markets and specialty shops looking for good locally made jams. Many vendors at the farmer's markets let you try their jams before you purchase. Aunt Polly's Pantry, in Rockland, Maine makes great jams and jellies, especially a Cabernet Sauvignon Wine jelly. She sells them at the Camden Farmer's Market on Saturdays, and lets you taste her jellies on crackers. Delicious!

$3/4$ cup salted butter, softened
$2/3$ cup sugar
1 egg
2 teaspoons vanilla
2 cups flour
$1/2$ teaspoon baking powder
Jelly

Cream the butter and sugar until light and fluffy. Beat in the egg and vanilla.

Stir in the flour and baking powder.

Preheat the oven to 350°F.

Cut the dough into quarters. Using your hands, roll each quarter into a log about 12 inches long. Place two of the logs on a baking sheet. Using your finger, make an indentation down the center of each log; fill with jelly. Bake the logs for 20 minutes. The logs should cook but not brown. While warm, cut the logs diagonally into cookies. Repeat with the other two logs.

Makes 4 dozen cookies

Strawberries and Honey

Marcia Gardiner maintains twelve beehives in the Belfast, Maine, area. She makes great-tasting honey from the nectar of flowers over three seasons. Spring honey has a very fruity flavor, as it comes from the flowers of blueberries, raspberries, strawberries, apples, pears, and peaches. Summer honey has a mildly sweet flavor from the nectar of roses, petunias, lavender, lilies, marigolds, and flowers from vegetables such as tomatoes, cucumbers, and squashes. (Marcia maintains one beehive near a farmer's vegetable field just for its honey.) Fall honey is rather dark with a stronger taste, as it comes from goldenrod, sumac, and wildflowers. Marcia sells her honey at the Belfast and Camden farmer's markets and from her home in Swanville.

Marcia's favorite dessert is fresh spring strawberries drizzled with her honey, and it has become one of our favorite desserts, too.

About the Author

With a bachelor's degree in home economics from Keene State College, New Hampshire and coursework at Madeleine Kamman's Modern Gourmet Boston, the San Francisco Culinary Academy, and the Culinary Institute of America, Joan Styrna has been both a chef and a teacher. Her life has centered on preparing good food for family, friends, and clients as well as teaching middle and high school students how to prepare good food. Through the Timberlane Regional School District in Plaistow, New Hampshire, Joan has worked many years developing a culinary arts program, writing and teaching an extensive curriculum.

Experiencing life as an adventurous journey, Joan is happiest when exploring the back roads of New England, hiking through the woods of Maine, and cooking for family and friends.

Joan lives in Brentwood, New Hampshire from September through June. In July and August, she lives her "dream life" in a cabin on Swan Lake in Maine.

About the Illustrator

Sheila Chambers Lemieux is a paraprofessional/LNA in a multi-handicapped, special education program. She was born and raised in Haverhill, Massachusetts, and now lives in Danville, New Hampshire, with her husband, Michael, and their four children, Aubrey, Shanoah, Seth, and Jacob.

# Index

Sally Dyer's Pickles, 101
San Francisco Cheesecake, 150

Sauces

barbecue sauce for spare
    ribs, 181
homemade applesauce, 30
tomato sauce, 138

Sauerkraut and Pork, 40
Sausage Soup, 163
Smoked Salmon Pâté, 208

Soups

cabbage soup, 6
cold beet soup, 215
cream of artichoke soup, 164
fourth of July at Swan Lake
    clam chowder, 212
hot beet soup, 8
sausage soup, 163

Sour Cherry Nut Cake, 78
Spaetzle, 140
Spanish Rice, 96
Spinach Salad with Chutney
    Dressing, 142
St. Patrick's Day Gelatin Salad, 188
Strawberries and Honey, 233
Strawberry Rhubarb Pudding
    Cake, 74
Stuffed Pepper Steaks, 46
Summer Vegetable Juice, 221
Summers in Maine, 201
Swiss Steak, 50
Teaching at Timberlane, 159
Thanksgiving Sage Bread Stuffing,
    62
The Best Blueberry Scones, 197
Tomato Sauce, 138

Tuna-Noodle Casserole, 58

Vegetables

babka, savory potato cake, 14
baked mashed potatoes, 57
baked onions, 64
cabbage soup, 6
chicken-wrapped stuffed
    poblano peppers, 173
chlodnik, 18
cold beet soup, 215
corn, tomato and avocado
    salsa, 222
cream of artichoke soup, 164
crêpe salsa, 132
eggplant frittata, 166
fried potatoes, 16
Grandpa's stuffed cabbage
    rolls, 10
guacamole, 133
hot beet soup, 8
making fresh sauerkraut, 42
mashed potato patties, 57
Mom's maple baked beans, 60
Mom's potato salad, 68
Mrs. Foster's broccoli salad, 98
my mother's coleslaw, 66
potato teasers, 218
sauerkraut and pork, 40
spinach salad with chutney
    dressing, 142
summer vegetable juice, 221
tomato sauce, 138
zucchini pancakes, 216

Vidalia Onion Marmalade, 183
Vinaigrette, 144
Yakatori, 134
Zucchini Pancakes, 216